Stress Free
COOKING

Stress Free…

1st printing, August 2002
ISBN: 0-9719776-0-7

WIMMER
COOKBOOKS

ConsolidatedGraphics

1-800-548-2537

Table of Contents

Dedication

For Mom & Dad who couldn't have given more
For Dave & Adam who couldn't mean more
For Alan who gently encourages more

Acknowledgements

This book would not have been such a joy without the help and encouragement of the following friends, family, mentors, and recipe testers (listed alphabetically):

Grace Albrecht
Kristin Albrecht
Jamaine Bell
Stephanie Blanchard
Jill Brandes
Richard Brightman
Kathy Clarkson
Ginny Conn
Kathy Coyne
Carole DeFillipis
Gina DeNapoli
Felice DeGuglielmo
Ann Hall Every, CCP
June C Jacobs, CCP
Kings Cookingstudios
The Kitchen Shoppe

Ann Lesnewich
Denise Todd Loretti
Sophia Martins
Lynda Miller
Beverly Mortenson
Rose Neubauer
Anita Nurge
Jan O'Brien
Kathy O'Shea
Janet Ricciardi
Aimee Ruzicka
Bill Seelig
Jennifer Seelig
Lillian Seelig
Sheila Thomas

All of my students

Stress Free
Pantry,
Equipment,
Variables

The Keys to a Stress Free Cooking Experience

There are many keys that I would like to share with you so that you can easily unlock the secrets of successful *Stress Free Cooking.* I want you to love and enjoy cooking as much as I do!

First, a well-planned, well-stocked pantry, refrigerator, and freezer are paramount to a new world of culinary enjoyment for you, your family, and friends. If you plan your market trips wisely, you will spend less time shopping-thus allowing more time for cooking. A basic pantry list, that doubles as a shopping list, is provided in this chapter to ensure that you can prepare fast, healthy, *Stress Free* meals. Please photocopy the list and take it with you to the market. By keeping these items on hand you will be able to make any recipe in this book on a moment's notice and in less time than it takes to pick up take out!

Good quality olive oils and vinegars are like fine wines and different ones appeal to different people. Some extra virgin olive oils taste peppery, some lemony, and yet some will taste grassy. Taste oils and vinegars and see which ones you like. Those will be the ones for your shopping list. Find the one(s) you like and keep them on hand. There is no right or wrong answer as far as flavor is concerned; however, there are health benefits that are achieved by selecting olive or canola oils. Both oils are polyunsaturated, or "Heart Healthy," and provide essential fatty acids, unlike butter which is saturated and contains cholesterol, or margarine with its trans fatty acids. Flavored oils can be used as condiments to finish a simple dish.

The same will hold true for herbs and spices. You may love a particular ingredient, while your spouse, partner, or children may not. You will become comfortable using herbs and spices once you have found your favorites. Herbs and spices can help you cut the fat calories in your cooking because they add strong flavors that replace the missing fats.

Pantry

Oils – a variety such as olive, extra virgin olive, and canola

Vinegars – a variety such as balsamic, red wine, champagne, and rice

Nonstick cooking spray

Sea salt – fine grind

Garlic – fresh, whole heads

Onions

Shallots

Whole peppercorns and a good quality pepper mill

All-purpose flour

Honey

Light brown sugar

Granulated sugar

Pasta – a variety of shapes and sizes

Rice – Jasmine, Arborio

Beans – canned, a variety to include: black beans, pink beans, chickpeas, and small white beans

Lentils – DePuy, brown, and red

Polenta/cornmeal

Evaporated skim milk

Canned broth and stock-chicken, beef, mushroom, and vegetable

Canned tomatoes – diced, crushed, and paste

Clams

Black olive paste

Capers

Olives

Canned fruits – such as Mandarin oranges, apricots, and crushed pineapple

Dried fruits – such as raisins and cherries

Freezer

Filled pastas-such as tortellini and agnolotti

Artichokes

Baby corn

Peas

String beans – whole

Pearl onions

Ground beef

Ground turkey

Chicken breasts – boneless, skinless, and individually wrapped

Roasting chickens, 5 to 6 pounds each

Large shrimp – cooked, peeled, and deveined

Large shrimp – uncooked, peeled, and deveined

Individually frozen fish fillets-such as whiting and halibut

Blueberries, raspberries, and strawberries

Pignoli nuts

Crêpes

Refrigerator

Lowfat cottage cheese

Light cream cheese (also labeled Neufchatel)

Mozzarella – in 1 pound blocks

Parmigiano – Reggiano

Eggs – large

Flour tortillas

Mustard – a variety such as smooth Dijon, stone ground, champagne, and honey

Vermouth – dry white

Wine – dry white

Salsas

Lemons and limes

Salad greens – in a variety of types, textures, and colors

Baby spinach

Carrots

Celery

Fresh herbs – basil, oregano, and rosemary

Sun-dried tomatoes (not in oil)

Additional items – your favorites

By keeping these items on hand, you will be able to come home from a busy day, put together a quick, delicious meal in no time and actually enjoy doing it.

Cook's Tips

You will find cook's tips for timesaving and efficiency noted on the appropriate recipes but I also thought it would be handy for you to have an overview in this chapter. The first tip is a result of a memorable experience at home. It was a hot summer day. My son Adam and his cousin Todd came bounding into the kitchen quickly searching for a cool refreshing drink. They opened the cupboard, grabbed two tall glasses, furiously opened the frig, found the juice pitcher and filled the huge glasses with ice-cold liquid. Todd began to wince. Adam exclaimed that there must be something wrong with the juice. They had in fact, mistaken the pitcher of chicken stock for a pitcher of apple juice. All of this happened so quickly that I wasn't able to stop them. The lesson I learned was to always label things in the frig.

- Purchase stock in large containers and keep the extra handy in the refrigerator for up to 10 days. If using a household juice pitcher, make sure you label and date it.

- Read the recipe thoroughly before cooking anything.

- Prepare a Mise En Place (p. 9).

- Cook twice as much pasta or rice as you need for one meal. Place the leftover, unsauced pasta (or rice) in a plastic bag and use within the week.

- Prepare basic sauces. You can achieve many sauces from one recipe simply by varying the type of stock or herbs found in the sauce. For instance, the Mushroom Sherry Sauce (p.20) in this book goes well with chicken or beef so you can use either stock to vary the sauce accordingly.

- When reading a recipe and the need to switch from fresh herbs to dry arises, the conversion is 1 part fresh to 3 parts dry.

- Chop enough fresh parsley to last from several days to one week. Parsley adds a fresh flavor and color to many dishes.

- Use a convection oven to roast and bake. Convection ovens generally cook foods in at least 25% less time than conventional.

- Roast a chicken one day and use the leftover chicken again in another type of dish later in the week.

- Make two meals that freeze well when you have extra cooking time. Eat one today and freeze the other.

- Use your crockpot to cook soups, stews, and sauces while you are out.

- Don't guess doneness - use a meat thermometer and you will not overcook as many expensive food items.

- Make enough salad dressing to last for several days.

- Wash and dry enough salad greens and fresh herbs to last for several days. Thorough drying keeps them fresh longer.

- Preserve leftover fresh herbs. Place the herbs in your food processor and mince. Add enough olive oil to make a paste and freeze in small plastic bags placed in a large plastic bag to keep them from getting lost in the freezer. These will be the base for your homemade salad dressing and seasonings for soups, stews, and sauces.

- Use an egg slicer to slice eggs, strawberries, olives and mushrooms.

- Grate several pounds of cheese, such as mozzarella or Cheddar. Place 1 cup of cheese in plastic sandwich bags and place these inside larger plastic bags in the freezer for quick use.

- Keep your knives sharp-they will make your work go more quickly.

- Use a larger bowl or pan than you think you will need so that you don't have to switch during the cooking process.

- Get the whole family involved for a fun family project.

Mise En Place

Make sure that you have all the recipe's ingredients and equipment on hand before you start the actual cooking. One thing that you can do to make your cooking the best it can be is to prepare a "mise en place" (MEEZ ahn plahs). Mise en place is a French term that refers to having all your ingredients in place and ready up to the point of cooking. By doing this you ensure that when you start any of the actual cooking, you will not have to stop at a critical point and hunt for an ingredient or the right knife to chop the garlic. Another great reason for having mise en place is in case of interruption. If one of the kids needs you or the phone or doorbell rings, you can go back to your cooking; and by having all the ingredients in place, you can determine quite easily where you left off.

The Right Equipment Makes All the Difference

Investing in good quality pots and pans is a great way to improve your culinary skills, but you should think carefully about what you are investing in. If you go and spend a small fortune on fine ingredients to create a meal and then spend your valuable time cooking them, you will want to make sure that you have the right tools to do your work justice. If you buy good quality pots and pans once, you will not likely have to buy another set later, so take your time and do your research when making a selection. If a certain cookware line appeals to you, try one piece and see if you like it before buying more.

Things to Consider When Selecting Cookware:

- What kind of cooking surface do you have? The ceramic or induction surfaces require a perfectly flat bottom to conduct heat efficiently.

- Is the equipment non-reactive? Stainless steel is non-reactive; aluminum is not. Tomatoes, citrus, and egg whites can react chemically in aluminum.

- Will you be able to pour easily from this pan? Flared sides or edges will help with this.

- Will the handles stay cool?

- Can the pan go from stovetop to oven?

- Is the pan constructed for fast responsiveness and even heating, without hot spots? Copper is the most efficient material but it is also very labor intensive to keep bright and shiny. However, you might consider buying a pan with a copper core.

- Do you need a non-stick surface? Most times, when cookware is of high quality and used properly, you will not need a non-stick pan.

- How will they clean? Will you want to put the pans in the dishwasher? Some exterior and nonstick finishes do not hold up well in the dishwasher. Copper exteriors, however, require special care.

- Do you need to purchase lids for each pot? You can purchase universal lids that fit several different pieces. Some lids are included with the purchase, however, so don't buy a lid that you won't need.

Basic equipment items to stock your kitchen:

- Grater and/or zester-such as the Microplane Greater/Zester
- Egg slicer for slicing eggs, mushrooms, and strawberries
- Flat meat pounder
- Parchment paper
- Salad spinner
- Instant read meat thermometer
- Pepper mill
- Mis en place dishes
  (small dishes for holding ingredients)
- Several sets of tongs for tossing salads and turning meat without piercing
- A graduated set of stainless steel and/or glass bowls
- Half sheet pans for baking cookies and roasting veggies

- 8-inch Chef's Knife
- 3 or 4-inch paring knife
- Serrated knife for soft items such as tomatoes and bread
- Fry or sauté pans – 8, 10 and 12-inch
- 4-quart Chef's Pan (also know as Saucier)
- Grill pan
- 3 and 4-quart saucepans
- 8-quart stock or soup pot
- Pizza stone
- Pizza peel
- Pizza wheel
- Dough scraper
- Food processor
- Immersion blender

My all time favorite pans are the Chef's pan and Braisers. The Chef's pan is a great all-purpose pot that can be used for cooking sauces, soups, stews, risotto, and even stir-fry. It has rounded sides so that stirring and whisking ingredients into this pan is a breeze. This is the pan you won't ever put away because you will use it so much, maybe everytime you prepare a meal. I also love Braisers (also known as Rondeau) because they can be used on the stovetop and then easily placed in the oven. It is easier and safer to lift with two loop handles, rather than one long one, particularly when full of food. They also have a domed lid that allows more flexibility than the flatter one that is more common to a fry pan.

Purchase your cookware from a reputable dealer who knows what they are selling and offers you the necessary education you need to make the appropriate purchase. Ask questions. Explain your needs and style of cooking.

Recipe Variables

Have you ever wondered why a recipe didn't turn out the way you had hoped? Please don't think you are alone; most of us can report some type of cooking disaster. Below are some helpful hints and interesting reasons why recipes fail.

The first rule of thumb when trying a new recipe is to read it through thoroughly. You don't want to get halfway through and find out that the dish has to cook for 2 hours when you were planning on eating in 20 or 30 minutes. Proper cooking time is essential. For example, rushing to cook a piece of meat will probably turn out a very tough product.

Second, is there a cooking method or term in the recipe that you don't understand? If so, check the Cook's Tips in this book so that you are prepared.

Just as everything else in life, there are variables in cooking and there are some that many people may never have occasion to think about. When recipes are developed, they are done so under a particular set of circumstances. The home cook will most likely be preparing it under a completely different set of circumstances. For instance, was the recipe developed in a professional kitchen or a home kitchen, was the stove gas or electric, what kind of equipment was used, and what was the atmosphere (humidity) in the kitchen? The quality of your pots and pans makes a huge difference in your cooking. More than likely, the circumstances in your kitchen will be different than that of the chef who developed the recipe. All of the recipes in this book were developed and tested in a home kitchen using a gas stove. All of these things will affect your finished product.

Many of my students express a lack of confidence in their own cooking. When I develop a recipe, I use my favorite things. These may not be yours or your family's favorites, so you might want to change a seasoning or two. That's ok. I want you to cook, not transform your taste buds to be the same as mine. Cooking is a way of expressing your love and care for your family and friends. We all have different tastes. What I want you to glean from my recipes is some culinary education, such as a new cooking method or a new ingredient to try. Then you can take the recipe and tailor it to your family's preferences. Cooking is an art, not an exact science. However, please be advised that baking is another story, there is science involved in baking.

Cooking with Wine

I don't want this to happen to you! Once when I was preparing to teach a cooking class, I was handed a bottle of white wine with a screw top and could not bring myself to use it with the fine quality of food that had been purchased for the class. Unfortunately, the clerk in the wine shop was not well versed in wine and sold this to the person marketing for the class. With a little know how, cooking with wine can be fun, adding depth, conducting flavor, and making your dishes more interesting. Just follow these guidelines:

- Cook with a wine that is drinkable. Even for cooking, the wine should have a cork!

- Cook with the same wine (grape variety) that you will be drinking with the meal. In other words, if you are cooking Italian and you will be serving Chianti with the meal, you will want to cook with Chianti or Sangiovese. Sangiovese is Chianti's California cousin, made from the same grape as Chianti, but cannot be called Chianti as that denotes the region in Italy where Sangiovese is turned into Chianti. You might not want to cook with a $20-40 bottle of wine, but you should at least choose a decent $10 bottle of the same variety. When selecting the wine for the meal, consider what is in the dish, as well as what the main food item is.

- Chardonnay is a difficult wine to cook with. There is a tendency for many Chardonnay wine makers to over-oak the wine. Cooking with Chardonnay would be like adding wooden splinters to your food instead of fine herbs. You may have heard the expression ABC, anything but Chardonnay, and this is why. Unfortunately, many Chardonnays have been poorly made and not dependable for cooking. Whites that are preferable are: Sauvignon blanc, pinot grigio or vermouth.

- Consider the type and strength of seasonings in the dish when selecting a wine. For example, fruity Zinfandels go well with highly spiced foods, Riojas with Mexican, and sweeter wines such as German Gewurztraminers or France's Alsatians go well with Asian food. Of course, you can always make exceptions and there will always be exceptions, so use the guidelines-but remember it is okay to enjoy your favorite wine with whatever you feel is appropriate.

Stress Free…

- Most wine experts feel that it is almost impossible to pair wine with artichokes. They contain a chemical called cynarin that stimulates the sweetness receptors in taste buds and makes everything taste exceptionally sweet for a short time. Cynar is so sweet that there was once talk of replacing sugar with it. There is an Italian aperitif called Cynar that is made from artichokes and similarly makes food taste sweeter. This is a good illustration of when it is necessary to match the wine with rest of the dish.

- Vermouth is a nice alternative to wine for cooking. If you don't generally keep wine on hand, try vermouth; it keeps for quite a long time in the refrigerator if tightly sealed-certainly longer than an open bottle of wine. It is extremely food friendly as it is a fortified wine made from 20 herbs and spices that vary depending on the brand that you select.

- It is also nice to keep the wines local; meaning that Italian wine is served with Italian food and French with French food, etc.

- Marinating with wine helps to tenderize the surface of the meat that it comes in contact with; but you will also need to add a healthy oil, such as extra virgin olive oil, to help the marinade penetrate the muscle and collagen. Marinating seafood for too long a period can actually toughen it, as it is tender to begin with.

- Wine is a conductor of flavor and therefore carries and enhances flavors in your cooking.

- Wine should be added in the early cooking stages so that the alcohol has time to evaporate from the dish.

- When adding alcohol to your cooking, please remove the pan from the heat so that there are no unwanted flare-ups.

As there are many wines to choose from, we have two choices before us: either shop in a reputable wine store where you trust the staff or do your own homework.

Now we are ready to begin cooking and have a wonderful, fulfilling *Stress Free* experience. You can also e-mail your questions to me at barbrseelig@nac.net.

Buon Appetito!

Stress Free
Basics

Vinaigrette

Yield: ¾ to 1 cup dressing   Equipment: wire whisk, medium sized mixing bowl

¼   cup vinegar
1   teaspoon Dijon mustard
    Pinch fine sea salt
    Freshly ground pepper, to taste
½-¾   cup extra virgin olive oil

- **Place vinegar, Dijon, salt and pepper in bowl. Start whisking and slowly stream in the olive oil. Taste after ½ cup has been added. The amount of oil required to balance the vinegar will depend on the vinegar selected.**

VARIATIONS:

Use different types and flavors of vinegar

Add 1 to 2 drops orange oil or orange extract

Add chopped fresh herbs

Add roasted garlic

COOK'S TIP:

Slowly whisking in the oil allows for a better emulsion.

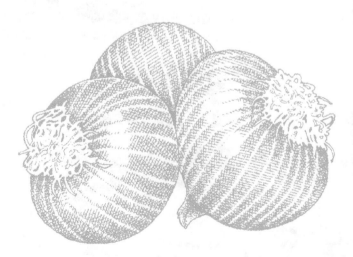

Pasta

Cooking pasta is very simple. The pasta must be cooked in lots of water so that it has room to dance in the pot. For best results just follow these simple guidelines.

Equipment: 8 to 10 quart stock pot with lid

1	pound pasta of your choice
8-10	quarts of boiling water
1	tablespoon fine sea salt

- **Bring water to rolling boil. Add salt.**

- **Add pasta and stir. Cover pan to help it return to a boil as quickly as possible.**

- **Once water returns to the boil you can remove lid. Stir to separate pasta.**

- **Cook to al dente stage, 9 to 11 minutes for dry pasta and 3 to 5 minutes for fresh pasta.**

COOK'S TIPS:

Al dente is an Italian phrase that means "to the tooth."
Pasta should be cooked until it gives slight resistance when bitten into.

You can make a double batch of pasta and save some for another meal by placing the drained, unsauced pasta in a large plastic bag and refrigerating it for up to 5 days.
There is no need to add oil. The oil will make the sauce slide off the pasta.
To reheat the leftover pasta, you can add it directly to the pan of hot sauce. See Pasta section.

Quick Marinara Sauce

Yield: 2 cups

Equipment: 10 to 12-inch sauté pan

Olive oil

4 cloves garlic, minced

½ cup chopped fresh basil

½ cup chopped oregano

12 fresh plum tomatoes, chopped

½ teaspoon fine sea salt

Freshly ground pepper

Additional basil as desired

- Pour enough olive oil in sauté pan to lightly film pan. Heat to medium.

- Add garlic and cook until fragrant.

- Add basil, oregano and tomatoes.

- Simmer 20 minutes.

- Add sea salt and pepper. Add more basil if desired. Simmer 10 minutes more.

Mashed Potatoes with No Cream or Butter

Serves 6 to 8   Equipment: electric mixer, colander placed in large bowl, saucepan

12   Yukon Gold potatoes, peeled and
         cut into 1-inch cubes
1   teaspoon fine sea salt
        Freshly ground pepper, to taste
4   cups chicken, vegetable or beef
         stock

- **Place potatoes, salt and pepper in heavy saucepan, add stock and additional water to cover.**

- **Boil until potatoes are fork tender.**

- **Drain liquid from potatoes into a bowl, and reserve liquid to add back to potatoes.**

- **Place potatoes in mixer bowl. Mix until smooth and add the hot cooking liquid until potatoes are desired consistency.**

HEALTHY NOTE:

You have saved all the vitamins and minerals by using the cooking liquid!
Also, by using the cooking water you will retain the potato starch,
which will add richness to the dish.

COOK'S TIP:

Leftover cooking liquid can be used in sauces or soups.

These potatoes can be frozen in an ovenproof casserole dish, defrosted
and reheated in a 350 degree oven until piping hot, approximately 45 minutes.

19

Mushroom Sherry Sauce

This wonderful sauce is very versatile and can be used on anything.

Equipment: 10 to 12-inch sauté pan.

2	tablespoons unsalted butter
1	shallot, minced
10	ounces mushrooms, sliced
2	tablespoons all-purpose flour
½	cup dry sherry
½-1	cup vegetable stock
½	cup Italian parsley, minced

- Melt butter in sauté pan over medium heat.
- Add shallots and mushrooms and cook until wilted.
- Add flour, mix well and cook 3 minutes.
- Add sherry and enough stock to achieve desired consistency.
- Add fresh parsley.
- Serve over any meat, fish or mashed potatoes.

VARIATIONS:

Use stock to complement your entrée.

Use wine or vermouth instead of sherry.

Hollandaise Sauce

Yield: 1½ cups   Equipment: 4 quart saucepan

2   tablespoons lemon juice
2   tablespoons melted butter
1   cup plain yogurt
½   teaspoon fine sea salt
2   eggs or 4 egg whites

- **Whisk all ingredients in a saucepan. Heat to medium and whisk until mixture barely begins to boil. Remove from heat.**

SERVING SUGGESTION:

Serve warm or chilled over well-drained vegetables or poached fish.

Poached Chicken Breast

Equipment: 10 to 12-inch sauté pan

4	boneless, skinless chicken breasts
1	carrot
1	stalk celery
1	bay leaf
2	quarts chicken stock or water

- Place chicken, carrot, celery and bay leaf in sauté pan and enough stock or water to completely cover chicken and bring to low boil.

- Reduce heat to low and cook 8 to 10 minutes.

- Cool chicken in stock and prepare as necessary for the desired recipe.

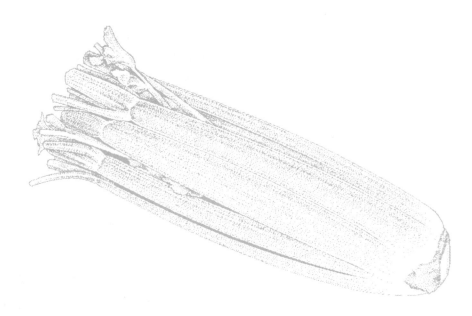

Risotto

Risotto must be served immediately. It does not wait!

Serves 4 as main course, 6 to 8 as first course

Equipment: 4 quart chef's pan or saucepan, additional 4 quart saucepan

---

4	cups stock
1½	cups dry white wine
	Extra virgin olive oil
1	cup sweet onion, chopped
2	cups Carnaroli or Arborio rice, checked over for imperfect grains
½	teaspoon fine sea salt
½	teaspoon freshly ground pepper
½	cup freshly grated Parmigiano-Reggiano
2	tablespoons finely minced Italian parsley leaves

- Bring stock and wine to a boil in 4 quart saucepan. Keep simmering on stove.

- Using a heavy 4 quart saucepan or chef's pan, thinly film the pan with olive oil and add onion. Sauté until onion starts to soften. Add rice and salt and pepper and coat rice grains with olive oil mixture. Add stock mixture 1 cup at a time and stir until each addition of liquid is absorbed. This takes time and patience. After last addition of stock is absorbed, add Parmigiano-Reggiano. When all stock is absorbed and rice grains are creamy you can add the parsley.

- Serve immediately.

Pizza

This dough makes 1 very large (16-inch) pie, 2 medium (8 to 10-inch) pies or 4 to 6 individual pizzas.

Equipment: food processor with steel blade, large work bowl, pizza stone, pizza peel or baking sheet without sides, pizza wheel, dough scraper

---

1¼	cup tepid water - using a meat or candy thermometer, the water should measure 110 to 120 degrees.
1	package or 2¼ teaspoons dry yeast (Rapid Rise is not necessary)
3½	cups all-purpose flour, plus extra for your work surface
1	hearty pinch of fine grind sea salt
1	tablespoon olive oil, plus extra for coating the dough during the rising process
	Cornmeal for sprinkling on the pizza peel

Toppings:

2	cups Quick Marinara Sauce or commercial pizza sauce
2	cups shredded mozzarella
	Additional items such as sliced mushrooms, pepperoni, etc.

- Mix yeast in tepid water. Let stand 5 to 10 minutes until foamy.

- Set up food processor with steel blade (an electric mixer fitted with a dough hook also works well). Pour flour and salt into food processor. Pulse 2 to 3 times to mix salt and flour well.

- Add yeast mixture and process until a ball forms inside the work bowl. Add 1 tablespoon extra virgin olive oil. Process 2 minutes.

- Dough should not be sticky. If it is you can add more flour. Add the flour ¼ cup at a time until dough is no longer sticky and does not stick to your hands.

- Remove from work bowl and place on work surface that is lightly sprinkled with flour. Knead 3 to 5 minutes until dough is as soft as a baby's bottom. Place dough in a lightly oiled bowl and turn to coat all sides. Cover with plastic wrap and set in a warm place to rise. Dough should double in size within 1 or 2 hours.

- Punch down and let rest for 10 minutes. Dough can also be given a second 1 hour rise for an even lighter pizza crust.

- Prepare pan: To avoid sticking, lightly sprinkle pan with cornmeal or line with parchment paper. If using a pizza peel to transfer pizza to stone, lightly sprinkle the peel with cornmeal.

Pizza continued

To cook pizza:

* Preheat oven and pizza stone to 500 degrees. Stretch dough to desired size on pizza peel or prepared pan. Add toppings. Reduce oven temperature to 400 degrees and bake until outside edges of crust are golden and cheese is bubbly, approximately 15 to 20 minutes.

VARIATIONS:

Grilled Pizza: Preheat grill at high for 10-15 minutes. Flatten dough to desired size. Do not add toppings yet. Reduce heat to medium. Place flattened pizza dough directly onto grate and cook approximately 3 to 5 minutes with cover closed, or until grill marks appear and you are able to turn pizza dough with tongs. Turn dough and add toppings. Cook another 5 minutes or so with lid down.

Toppings for grilled pizza should generally be light and can include fresh sliced tomatoes, fresh basil from your herb garden, and fresh mozzarella. You can also top your pizza with dollops of ricotta and homemade basil olive oil paste. (see Basics).

COOK'S TIPS:

The moisture content in your flour and the atmosphere in your kitchen can vary greatly each time you make pizza. The best way to judge the dough is by the feel. It should feel smooth and not at all sticky.

Let pizza rest 5 to 10 minutes before cutting.

You can make pizza dough ahead and either let it rise all day in the refrigerator or freeze it.

A damp tea towel will also work in place of plastic wrap if you are placing your dough in a warm oven (less than 200 degrees) to rise. A hot, humid, summer day is great for rising. On top of a warm oven is also a good place to put dough to rise.

Roasted Garlic

Equipment: heavy duty aluminum foil, ceramic basking dish

4   large heads of garlic
     Olive oil
     Fine sea salt
     Freshly ground pepper

- Preheat oven to 400 degrees.

- Using chef's knife, slice a thin piece off the top or stem end of the garlic to expose most of the cloves.

- Place heads on large sheet of aluminum foil and drizzle with just enough olive oil to moisten the garlic, approximately ½ teaspoon per head. This will vary depending on the size of the garlic.

- Sprinkle with a dash of sea salt and freshly ground pepper.

- Wrap up tightly and place in ceramic dish. Bake approximately 45 minutes or until very soft to the touch and a spreadable consistency.

VARIATIONS:

Break cloves apart, drizzle with oil, season with salt and pepper and roast in foil 20 to 30 minutes.

Peel garlic cloves, drizzle with oil, season with salt and pepper and roast in foil 20 minutes.

Roasted Potatoes

Serves 4 to 6   Equipment: large baking sheet, parchment paper, garlic peeler

3   pounds potatoes such as Yukon
        gold or red bliss
2   tablespoons fresh rosemary
8   garlic cloves, whole, peeled
       Extra virgin olive oil
       Fine sea salt
       Freshly ground pepper

- **Preheat oven to 425 degrees.**

- **Wash and dry potatoes. Cut into bite-size pieces, if necessary.**

- **Strip rosemary from stems. Slightly bruise with chef's knife.**

- **Peel garlic.**

- **Set parchment paper in baking sheet. Place potatoes, rosemary and garlic on baking sheet. Drizzle with just enough olive oil to thinly film all potatoes.**

- **Toss with salt and pepper.**

- **Roast in oven 30 minutes to 1 hour or until fork tender and nicely browned.**

Roasted Vegetables

Equipment: large baking sheet, parchment paper

1   eggplant, unpeeled, cut into
        1-inch chunks (whatever color
        you like)
1   zucchini, sliced into 1-inch pieces
1   yellow squash, sliced into 1-inch
        pieces
10   ounces cremini mushrooms
4   shallots, peeled and quartered
1   red bell pepper cut into 1-inch
        chunks
1   green bell pepper cut into 1-inch
        chunks
1   yellow bell pepper cut into 1-inch
        chunks
1   head garlic, cloves separated and
        peeled
      Fine sea salt
      Freshly ground pepper
      Olive oil
      Good quality balsamic vinegar
      Fresh herb sprigs for garnish

- **Preheat oven to 425 degrees.**

- **Salt eggplant on both sides and let stand for 20 to 30 minutes. This will prevent it from absorbing too much oil.**

- **Line baking sheet with parchment. Place cut vegetables and garlic on baking sheet. Sprinkle with salt and pepper to taste. Drizzle with small amount of olive oil and toss, coating all vegetables lightly.**

- **Roast to desired doneness, approximately 20 to 30 minutes.**

- **Taste to adjust seasonings. Place on serving platter and sprinkle with balsamic vinegar. Garnish with fresh herbs.**

Stir-Fry Guidelines

- Make sure all knives are sharp

- Do all prep (cleaning, chopping) in advance, cut longer cooking vegetables into smaller pieces than quicker cooking items.

- Partially freeze meats to make slicing easier

- Marinate meat or fish. Fish 20 minutes, meat 1 to 2 hours.

- Assemble all ingredients in a mise en place.

- Heat wok or large sauté pan prior to adding oil and food.

- Add oil.

- Add foods in order of cooking time - slow cooking first, then quick cooking. Cook vegetables first, remove and then cook meat or fish.

- Add seasonings and combine meat, fish and vegetables.

- Sauces can be thickened by adding a mixture of liquid thickened with cornstarch. Basic recipe: 1 teaspoon cornstarch dissolved in ¼ cup water or stock. Cook until sauce is thickened and clear.

Stir-Fry with Seasonal Vegetables

This is a very flexible recipe. You can make this with chicken, shrimp, scallops, beef or pork. Select a stock that complements your protein.

Serves 4   Equipment: 10 to 12-inch sauté pan, chef's pan or wok

---

1   cup white wine

1   tablespoon complementary stock

1   pound of chicken, shrimp, scallops, beef or pork (see Cook's Tips below)

1   tablespoon cornstarch

1   cup stock

2   tablespoons peanut oil

2-3 cloves garlic, peeled and sliced

1   inch piece ginger, peeled and sliced

3   cups seasonal vegetables or your favorite vegetables, cut into bite-size pieces, (keeping in mind that longer cooking vegetables should be cut into smaller pieces)

2   cups cooked jasmine rice

- Prepare marinade: mix stock and wine. Place chicken, shrimp, scallops, beef or pork in marinade.

- Prepare sauce: mix 1 tablespoon of cornstarch with 1 cup stock. Set aside.

- Heat oil in a large sauté pan, chef's pan or wok.

- Add garlic and ginger and cook until golden. Remove.

- Add longer cooking vegetables first and work down to quicker cooking items.

- Push vegetables to the side of the pan. Drain marinade from meat and reserve. Add meat to pan and stir-fry until done.

- Mix reserved marinade with cornstarch mixture and add to stir-fry. Cook until sauce is thickened and serve over jasmine rice.

COOK'S TIP:

Chicken, pork, and beef should be thinly sliced. Shrimp should be peeled and deveined.

Sauté Guidelines

- Sauté - To cook food quickly in a small amount of fat.

- Use naturally tender cuts of meat, which are uniform in size and shape.

- Foods may be finished in an oven after starting on the range top.

- Thinly film sauté pan with oil or spray.

- Preheat pan until hot, but not smoking, to ensure proper color and flavor.

- Place the most attractive side of food in the pan first to achieve the best presentation.

- Turn food only once to avoid excessive loss of flavor and juices.

- Remove food from pan and deglaze with water, stock or wine to release accumulated food. This is the basis for a sauce.

- Finish sauce as desired while keeping sautéed food warm.

Sautéed Baby Spinach

This dish adds so much to simple entrees in no time! It is lovely in place of a salad or as a bed upon which you can place a piece of grilled chicken.

Equipment: 10-inch sauté pan

2	garlic cloves, minced
½	cup chicken or vegetable stock
1	(10-ounce) bag baby spinach
1	teaspoon fine sea salt
	Freshly ground pepper

- Rinse spinach and drain well.

- Place ½ cup stock in sauté pan. Add garlic and cook fragrant.

- Add spinach and sauté until wilted.

- Season with salt and freshly ground pepper to taste.

VARIATIONS:

Add a splash of balsamic vinegar, a squeeze of lemon juice or
a teaspoon of grated orange zest once spinach is cooked.

Stress Free
Appetizers

Asparagus Crêpes with Fresh Herb Cheese

The crêpe batter needs a 30 minute to 24 hour resting period. Crêpes can be made ahead and frozen or refrigerated.

Yield: 24   Equipment: mixing bowl, nonstick crêpe pan or
small sauté pan, rubber spatula, parchment or waxed paper

For Basic Crêpes: (to make 2 dozen 4-inch crêpes)

1	large egg
2	large egg whites
1	cup 2% milk
⅓	cup water
2	tablespoons unsalted butter, melted
1	cup unbleached, all-purpose flour
¼	teaspoon fine sea salt

For Filling:

1	(8-ounce) brick Neufchâtel cream cheese (light cream cheese)
¼	cup fresh chives, chopped
¼	cup flat Italian parsley, chopped
24	thin asparagus spears

COOK'S TIP:

Crêpes can be prepared up
to 1 day ahead or frozen for 2 weeks.
Wrap tightly in plastic.

- For filling: Bring cream cheese to room temperature.

- Mix cream cheese and herbs for filling. Set aside.

- For crêpes: Whisk together eggs, egg whites, milk, water and melted butter. Whisk in the flour and salt until all lumps have disappeared. Place in an airtight container. Refrigerate 30 minutes to 24 hours.

- Wash asparagus and break ends off at point which they snap. Steam for 6 minutes. Remove from steamer and place in a bowl of ice cold water to preserve color and prevent further cooking.

- To make crêpes: Heat pan. Pour 2 tablespoons of batter in center and swirl around to make thin crêpe. Cook until top is dry, approximately 1 minute. Using a rubber spatula, flip crêpe to cook other side. Crêpe will slide off pan when ready. Place on paper towel and repeat. Place paper towels between crêpes.

- Assemble: Cut asparagus to appropriate length for crêpes. Layer 1 crêpe, ½ to 1 teaspoon cheese mixture and one asparagus spear.

- Roll up and serve with additional fresh herb garnish.

Basil Cups with Roasted Red Pepper and Fresh Mozzarella

This appetizer/hors d'oeuvre is easy to prepare, colorful, and can be made early in the day.

Equipment: cutting board, chef's knife, large platter

1	pound fresh mozzarella
1	bunch fresh basil, washed and dried (large leaves are best)
4	roasted red peppers
2	cans rolled anchovies with capers (optional)
	Good quality extra virgin olive oil (optional)
	Freshly ground pepper

- **Cut mozzarella and red pepper in 1-inch squares.**

- **Layer a basil leaf, a piece of mozzarella, a piece of roasted red pepper and top with a rolled anchovy.**

- **Cover and refrigerate until serving time.**

VARIATION:

If you do not like anchovies, drizzle the serving dish with good quality extra virgin olive oil and a light grinding of fresh pepper.

35

Clams in Fennel and Tomato Broth

Don't waste any of this broth; make sure you have a good bread to sop it all up.

Serves 2   Equipment: chef's pan with lid

1	fennel bulb, sliced thinly from tip to core
	Fresh basil, 4 large stems with leaves
	Fresh oregano, 4 large stems with leaves
1	lemon, sliced
4	plum tomatoes, chopped
	Dash of sea salt
	Freshly ground pepper
2	dozen cherrystone clams or 2 pounds of mussels, scrubbed
2	cups dry white wine such as Pinot Grigio

- Layer all ingredients in a chef's pan as follows:
  Fennel
  Herbs
  Lemon
  Tomatoes
  Salt and pepper
  Clams or mussels
  Wine

- **Cover. Bring to a boil and steam until clams open.**

- **Serve in bowls with crusty Italian bread and extra broth.**

Herb, Garlic and Lemon Chickpea Dip

This dip is similar to hummus but I left out the tahini (sesame paste) which is almost all fat and can be costly and not readily available. It also has a brighter, fresher flavor since the garlic and lemon are more noticeable.

Yield: 2½ cups   Equipment: food processor fitted with steel blade

---

2   cups canned chickpeas, drained
        and rinsed well

2   cloves garlic, crushed and peeled

2   lemons, juiced

2   teaspoons cumin

1   tablespoon olive oil

    Fine sea salt

    Freshly ground pepper

¼   cup chopped Italian parsley

1   tablespoon chopped fresh chives

- **Mix all ingredients, except parsley and chives, in a food processor to make a smooth paste. Remove from food processor and stir in fresh herbs.**

- **Can be prepared up to 2 days ahead.**

SERVING SUGGESTION:

Suitable as a dip for pita chips and raw vegetables
or as a spread for grilled vegetable sandwiches.

COOK'S TIP:

To crush and peel garlic at the same time, you can place it on a cutting
board and crush it with the side of a large chef's knife or a flat meat pounder.

Portobello Crostini with Balsamic Glaze

Equipment: pastry brush, 10 to 12-inch sauté pan, grill pan (optional)

1 loaf Italian bread, sliced ½-inch on the diagonal

Olive oil

2 cups onion, thinly sliced

2 garlic cloves, minced

6 portobello mushrooms, sliced ¼-inch thick

Fine sea salt

Freshly ground pepper to taste

Crushed red pepper to taste (optional)

¾ cup balsamic vinegar

- Brush bread with olive oil and grill or broil until golden. Can be done a day ahead and placed in plastic bag.

- Heat a sauté pan and thinly film with olive oil. Add onion, garlic and mushrooms. Cook until soft and onions are translucent. Add salt and pepper to taste and red pepper, if desired. Can also be done a day ahead and reheated or brought to room temperature before serving.

- Heat balsamic vinegar in a small saucepan and reduce until syrupy. This will take approximately 20 minutes. Set aside.

- Spread mushroom mixture on grilled bread.

- Drizzle with reduced balsamic vinegar.

- Can be served as an appetizer or hors d'oeuvre.

COOK'S TIP:

Keep all components separate and assemble at serving time.

Onion Herb Crisps

These crispy herb d'oeuvres are great with drinks or a glass of wine!

Equipment: food processor, baking sheets, parchment paper, pastry brush

¼   pound reduced fat, sharp, New York Style Cheddar cheese, shredded

3   tablespoons unsalted butter, cut into thirds

1   teaspoon onion flakes

1   teaspoon Italian Herb Blend

½   teaspoon hot pepper sauce

½   teaspoon fine sea salt

1   cup unbleached flour

1   teaspoon baking powder

2   egg whites

½   teaspoon sea salt

    Olive oil

- Preheat oven to 350 degrees.
- Line baking sheets with parchment.
- Place cheese, butter, onion flakes, Italian Herb blend, hot pepper sauce, and salt in the work bowl of your food processor. Blend well.
- Add flour and baking powder and pulse just until flour is blended in. This will look like coarse corn meal. Stream in just enough olive oil to bind.
- Form into 2 logs and place on plastic wrap. Roll tightly and refrigerate at least 30 minutes.
- Slice into ¼-inch disks and place on prepared baking sheet.
- Mix egg white with salt for glaze. Brush glaze on each round.
- Bake until lightly browned, approximately 13 to 15 minutes.

COOK'S TIPS:

Dough can be frozen or crisps can be baked and frozen.
Do not let parchment extend beyond baking sheet or it will burn.

VARIATION:

Dough can also be rolled out to ¼-inch thickness
and cut with small, seasonal cookie cutters for a festive look.

Onion Tart

The golden brown of the onions is complemented by the rosemary.

Serves 6 to 8   Equipment: baking sheet, 8 to 10-inch sauté pan, parchment paper

1	piece frozen puff pastry or basic pizza dough
1	pound onions, cipollini preferred
	Olive oil
¼	cup rosemary leaves
½	cup freshly grated Parmigiano-Reggiano

- Defrost puff pastry according to package (allow 3 hours), or prepare recipe for basic pizza dough found in this book on p. 24.

- To peel onions: Fill a medium saucepan with water and heat water to boiling. Cut the stem end off the onions and drop into boiling water for 3 minutes or until skins will peel easily. Remove. Cool. Peel. Slice.

- Thinly film a large sauté pan with olive oil. Add onions and sauté until they begin to caramelize and soften.

- Lay pastry or pizza dough on baking sheet lined with parchment. Crimp edges of pastry to form an edge on the tart.

- Spread onions over pastry. Sprinkle with rosemary leaves and Parmigiano-Reggiano. Bake 15 minutes in 400 degree oven.

- Cut into small pieces and serve as appetizer or side dish.

- Can be served at room temperature or warm from the oven.

Quick Quesadilla

8	flour tortillas
1	cup shredded light Cheddar cheese
½	cup chopped fresh herbs such as cilantro, parsley, and chives

- Place tortillas on work surface and sprinkle half of each with cheese and herbs.

- Fold and place on baking sheet lined with parchment paper.

- Bake at 400 degrees for 10 minutes or until cheese is melted.

- Cut each quesadilla into 3 or 4 pieces and serve with salsa.

Salmon and Hearts of Palm on Endive

Equipment: chef's knife and serving dish

1	(8-ounce) brick Neufchâtel cream cheese (light cream cheese)
¼	cup fresh minced dill
1	lemon, juiced
3	heads Belgian endive
10	ounces canned hearts of palm
1	pound smoked salmon, thinly sliced
	Freshly ground pepper
	Extra dill sprigs for garnish

- Soften cream cheese at room temperature for approximately 20 minutes. Mix with minced dill and lemon juice.

- Wash and dry the endive. Separate the leaves (spears).

- Cut hearts of palm into quarters, lengthwise. Wrap lengthwise in a piece of salmon.

- To assemble: Spread a thin layer of the cream cheese mixture on the endive leaf and top with the salmon wrapped heart of palm.

- Garnish with a sprinkling of freshly ground black pepper and a piece of dill.

COOK'S TIP:

For do ahead entertaining:
Prep all ingredients including wrapping the hearts of palm,
wrap items separately so the endive does not wilt, and assemble just before serving.

Pan Seared Scallops with Bell Pepper Confetti

Serves 4 as an appetizer course   Equipment: 10 to 12-inch sauté pan

½	green bell pepper, ¼-inch dice
½	red bell pepper, ¼-inch dice
½	yellow bell pepper, ¼-inch dice
½	cup uncooked polenta or cornmeal
¼	teaspoon fine sea salt
	Freshly ground pepper
16	large sea scallops
	Olive oil
½	cup dry white wine

- Mix peppers together and set aside.

- Place polenta in large bowl. Season with salt and pepper. Dip scallops in polenta and coat all sides.

- Thinly film sauté pan with olive oil and heat to medium high.

- Add scallops and sear on one side. Add the bell peppers and sauté while cooking scallops. Turn scallops and brown other side.

- Remove scallops to serving plates.

- Add white wine to pan. The addition of the wine will deglaze the pan and release any bits that are sticking. This will create a nice light sauce.

- Sprinkle the scallops with the cooked bell peppers and sauce.

Seviche in a Pasta Shell

A seafood hors d'oeuvre in a seashell. Seviche is an interesting phenomenon. The scallops are "cooked" in the lime juice.

Yield: approximately 20

Equipment: glass or ceramic dish large enough to hold scallops in single layer, pasta pot, rubber gloves for seeding and mincing jalapeños

---

12	ounces bay scallops
1	cup freshly squeezed lime juice
½	cup finely chopped red onion
1	small ripe tomato, peeled and chopped
1-2	fresh jalapeños, seeded and finely minced (wear gloves)
¼	cup canola oil
1	teaspoon granulated sugar
2	tablespoons white wine vinegar
½	cup fresh cilantro leaves, coarsely chopped
	Fine sea salt
	Freshly ground white pepper
12	ounces large (not jumbo) pasta shells, cooked al dente

- Place scallops in a dish and add just enough lime juice to cover. Refrigerate at least 5 hours (not more than 24). Stir several times while in refrigerator.

- Add onion, tomato, jalapeño, oil, sugar, vinegar, cilantro to scallops and salt and pepper to taste. Toss gently. Cover and refrigerate until time to assemble.

- Cook pasta shells al dente. Drain and place in a large bowl of cold water for about 5 minutes. Drain again, cover with paper towels and place in refrigerator about 20 minutes.

- To assemble: Drain the seviche and spoon into the pasta shells. Arrange on a platter and garnish with more fresh cilantro.

Lemon Dill Shrimp on a Cucumber Flower

Yield: 20 to 24   Equipment: bowl for marinating, steamer basket and large pot with lid

1	pound medium shrimp, peeled and deveined (see Cook's Tip)
1	lemon, juiced
1	shallot, finely minced
¼	cup olive oil
½	cup chopped dill
15	ounces black olives, sliced
	Fine sea salt
	Freshly ground pepper
2	English cucumbers
	Dill sprigs for garnish

- Steam shrimp in large pot with steamer basket insert. Cook just until pink, about 5 to 6 minutes, or defrost frozen shrimp under cold running water.

- Mix lemon juice, shallot, olive oil, chopped dill, olives, and salt and pepper to taste. Marinate shrimp in this mixture for at least one hour and up to 24 hours.

- Scrub cucumber well. Take a fork and run it up and down the outside of cucumber to make a decorative edge. Slice cucumber into ¼-inch rounds.

- Place one piece of shrimp on a cucumber slice and garnish with another sprig of fresh dill. Cover and refrigerate until serving time.

COOK'S TIP:

Good quality frozen cooked, peeled and deveined shrimp can be used.
Don't forget to use your egg slicer for the olives or you can purchase sliced olives.

Shrimp and Goat Cheese Mousse on Endive Spears

Yield: 36 to 48 pieces

8	ounces goat cheese such as Montrachet
4	ounces Neufchâtel cheese, (light cream cheese)
2	tablespoons fresh dill, chopped
1	tablespoon freshly grated orange zest
½	pound medium shrimp, steamed, peeled and deveined
	Fresh dill for garnish
3-4	heads Belgium endive, washed and dried, leaves separated and kept whole

- Mix together goat cheese, cream cheese, dill and orange zest.

- Place a teaspoon of goat cheese mousse on the wider end of the endive.

- Top with a shrimp and a fresh sprig of dill.

- Refrigerate until serving time.

COOK'S TIP:

A spoon or a pastry bag with a large star tip can be used.

Spinach Dip with Basil

This recipe makes a very flavorful and really healthy low-fat dip or spread that your guests will not believe is so good for them!

Equipment: food processor fitted with steel blade

1	cup fresh baby spinach
2	cloves garlic, minced
1	tablespoon minced shallot, approximately 1 large
¼	cup grated Parmigiano-Reggiano
½	cup fresh basil
1	cup nonfat cottage cheese
2	teaspoons extra virgin olive oil
2	tablespoons skim milk (optional)

- Place spinach, garlic, shallot, Parmigiano-Reggiano and basil in food processor. Process to a paste.

- With motor running, add cottage cheese and oil. Process until smooth. Add milk to achieve the desired consistency for your use.

Cook's Tip:
Best when made a day ahead.

Notes

Stress Free
Brunch

Grilled Fruit Kabobs

Grilling fruit enhances the natural sugars.

Serves 6 to 8   Equipment: grill, wooden skewers

1	pineapple, cut into 1-inch chunks
2-3	bananas, cut into 1-inch chunks
1	Granny Smith apple, sliced into 8 pieces
2	navel oranges, sliced into ¼-inch rounds
½	cup honey
¼	teaspoon cinnamon
2	tablespoons fresh orange juice
	Wooden skewers, soaked at least 30 minutes in water
	Fresh mint for garnish

- Preheat grill.

- Thread assorted fruits on wooden skewers that have been soaked in water for at least 30 minutes. This will avoid charring.

- Mix together honey, cinnamon and orange juice. Brush on fruit.

- Grill until fruit is golden.

- Garnish with fresh mint.

Salmon and Chive Pinwheels

This recipe is a light alternative to lox and bagels.

Yield: 16 to 24 pieces

8   ounces smoked salmon, thinly sliced

4   ounces Neufchâtel cream cheese (light cream cheese)

2   tablespoons chives, snipped or chopped

1   loaf cocktail bread, pumpernickel or rye

Additional chives for garnish, chopped

- Lay salmon out so that you have 2 squares, approximately 4 ounces each. It is like making a puzzle.

- Mix cream cheese and chives together and spread ½ of this mixture on each square of salmon.

- Roll like a jelly roll and freeze for 30 minutes. This will make slicing easier.

- Slice ¼-inch thick and place on a piece of cocktail bread. Garnish with chopped fresh chives.

- Serve immediately or cover tightly and serve within a few hours.

Harvest Muffins

These muffins are a lovely addition to any meal and they are also a terrific Breakfast To Go.

Equipment: large mixing bowls, muffin tins, food processor with shredding disk

---

2½	cups whole wheat flour
1½	cups white flour
1	cup sugar
4	teaspoons baking soda
4	teaspoons cinnamon
½	teaspoon cloves
½	teaspoon nutmeg
4	cups finely chopped unpeeled apples, about 5
1	cup finely chopped unpeeled carrots, about 3
1	cup raisins
2	cups nonfat yogurt
½	cup skim milk
4	teaspoons vanilla extract
4	whole eggs or 8 whites
	Nonstick cooking spray

- **Preheat oven to 350 degrees.**

- **Combine dry ingredients in a 4 quart bowl.**

- **Shred apples and carrots in a food processor with a shredding disk.**

- **Add apples, carrots, and raisins to dry ingredients.**

- **Mix wet ingredients and add to dry.**

- **Spray muffin pan and bake as follows:**

   Mini - 20 minutes, yield 72

   Regular - 25 to 30 minutes, yield 36

   Large - 35 to 45 minutes, yield 18

COOK'S TIPS:

These muffins keep well but must be refrigerated or frozen after 1 day due to the yogurt. These muffins are very moist so you don't need to line the muffin tins with bake cups. If you choose to line the muffin tins, aluminum, rather than paper bake cups are suggested, however, simply spraying the muffin pans works best.

SERVING SUGGESTION:

For Breakfast to Go, freeze muffins in individual baggies.

Breakfast Spread

Serve on your favorite bagels, muffins, waffles or pancakes.

Yield: 1¼ cups

½	cup low-fat ricotta cheese
½	cup chopped fresh fruit-berries, bananas, apples
¼	cup raisins or chopped dried fruit
2	teaspoons honey

- **Mix all ingredients in a small bowl.**

VARIATION:

Use your favorite fresh or dried fruit.

COOK'S TIP:

Best made several hours ahead so that flavors can blend.

53

Strawberry Banana Stuffed French Toast

This is an elegant, easy, make ahead brunch dish for the holidays. My husband and I had a higher fat version at The Franconia Inn in Franconia, New Hampshire and I just had to come home and make it healthier!

Serves 4 to 6   Equipment: 9 x 13-inch casserole dish

1	loaf unsliced dense bread, such as Challah
1	pint strawberries, chopped
1	banana, chopped
12	ounces whipped cream cheese
	Nonstick cooking spray
1	cup maple syrup
4	eggs or equivalent egg whites
1½	cups skim milk
2	teaspoons vanilla extract
¾	teaspoon ground nutmeg

- Slice bread about 1½-inch thick. Cut a pocket in each slice.

- Mix fruit and cream cheese. Stuff each pocket with this mixture.

- Spray a 9 x 13-inch pan with nonstick cooking spray. Pour maple syrup into bottom of pan.

- Lay stuffed bread on top of syrup.

- Mix eggs, milk, vanilla, and nutmeg. Pour over bread.

- Refrigerate several hours or overnight.

- Bake at 350 degrees for approximately 30 minutes until golden.

Omelets To Order

Serves 4   Equipment: 10 to 12-inch nonstick sauté pan

1	whole egg
2	egg whites
	Dash fine sea salt
	Freshly ground pepper
	Olive oil
¼	cup chopped onion
½	cup sliced mushrooms

- **Scramble eggs in a large bowl. Add sea salt and a few grindings of fresh pepper.**

- **Thinly film sauté pan with olive oil. Heat.**

- **Sauté onions and mushrooms. Remove and set aside.**

- **Add egg mixture and cook until almost set.**

- **Return vegetables to center of eggs. Fold over and continue to cook until eggs are done.**

VARIATIONS:

Vary the number of whole eggs depending on your needs.

Use your favorite vegetables.

COOK'S TIPS:

Two egg whites are the equivalent of one whole egg.

A nonstick pan really helps when making an omelet but if you don't have one,
you can lightly spray your pan with nonstick cooking spray and watch
it very carefully, cooking on low to medium.

Savory Breakfast Casserole

This dish is excellent for large groups and can be made ahead because it freezes beautifully.

Serves 6 to 8   Equipment: 9 x 13-inch ovenproof casserole, whisk, large mixing bowl

---

	Nonstick cooking spray
8	large eggs or equivalent combination of eggs and egg whites
½	teaspoon fine sea salt
¼	teaspoon freshly ground pepper
2	cups skim milk
1	teaspoon Dijon mustard
1	pound breakfast sausage, cooked and crumbled
3	thick slices good quality bread, torn into 2-inch pieces
1	cup low-fat shredded Cheddar cheese

- **Spray casserole dish with nonstick spray.**

- **Place eggs, salt and pepper in a large mixing bowl. Beat well.**

- **Add milk and mustard. Beat well.**

- **Place crumbled sausage and torn bread in bottom of casserole dish. Pour egg milk mixture over. Sprinkle with cheese.**

- **Cover and refrigerate several hours.**

- **Preheat oven to 350 degrees.**

- **Bake 30 to 40 minutes or until set. Casserole will be puffed in the center.**

- **Cut into squares and serve hot.**

COOK'S TIPS:

Reheats well in microwave.

Vegetarian breakfast sausage is also suitable.

Asparagus with Hollandaise Sauce

Serves 4 to 6   Equipment: 4 quart saucepan, vegetable steamer

2   pounds asparagus, washed and
     trimmed

Hollandaise Sauce: (Yield: 1½ cups)
2   tablespoons lemon juice
2   tablespoons melted butter
1   cup plain yogurt
½   teaspoon fine sea salt
2   eggs or 4 egg whites

- Steam asparagus to desired tenderness.

- Whisk all ingredients in a saucepan. Heat to medium and whisk until mixture barely begins to boil. Remove from heat.

- Serve warm or chilled over asparagus.

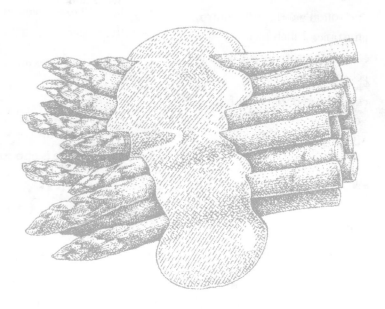

Mango Chicken Salad with Jicama

This refreshing salad has a surprise crunch from the diced jicama. The mango adds its own heavenly sweetness and lots of Vitamin C.

Equipment: cheesecloth or coffee filter, strainer, bowl

8	ounces plain low-fat yogurt
2	chicken breasts, poached, cooled and diced (see recipe for Poached Chicken Breast, p. 22)
3	cups chicken stock
¼	cup finely minced red onion
1	large mango, diced into ¼-inch pieces
½	cup jicama, diced into ¼-inch pieces
1	cup roughly chopped cilantro
1	lime, juiced
	Fine sea salt, to taste
	Freshly ground pepper
4	cups mixed greens, washed and dried
	Additional mango and cilantro for garnish
½	cup toasted sunflower, pumpkin seeds or soy nuts for garnish

- Drain yogurt through a cheesecloth or coffee filter placed in a strainer which has been placed in a bowl to reduce whey and make thicker consistency.

- Mix chicken, red onion, mango, jicama, cilantro, lime juice and ½ the yogurt. Blend well. Add remaining yogurt as necessary for desired consistency. Add salt and pepper to taste.

- Serve over mixed greens and garnish with additional mango, seeds and cilantro.

SERVING SUGGESTION:

This dish also makes a lovely hors d'oeuvre if placed in
phyllo tart shells. For tart shells see recipe for Apple Tarts (p. 146).

Black Bean and Sweet Potato Hash

This recipe can be served as a brunch item, a side dish to a simple grilled meat or a vegetarian entrée.

Serves 4 to 6   Equipment: 10 to 12-inch nonstick sauté pan

6	slices turkey bacon cut into 1-inch pieces
½	cup chopped onion
1	large bell pepper, yellow or green, cut into ½-inch dice
4	cups diced sweet potatoes, unpeeled, approximately 4 medium
	Fine sea salt
15	ounces canned black beans, drained and rinsed well
	Freshly ground pepper

- **Microwave potatoes until almost tender.**

- **In sauté pan, cook bacon, onion, bell pepper, potatoes and a pinch of sea salt over medium high heat until vegetables are tender and browned. Add beans and cook 5 minutes.**

- **Season with pepper.**

- **Keep warm until ready to serve.**

SERVING SUGGESTION:

Can be served with French toast, poached eggs or
the Omelet to Order included in this chapter.

HEALTHY NOTE:

Carefully read all packages of turkey bacon to find the
lowest fat version. There is a broad range of fat content.

Ricotta and Fresh Fruit Parfait

A refreshing finish to a satisfying brunch.

Serves 4   Equipment: food processor with steel blade

15	ounces part-skim ricotta cheese
¼	cup honey
1	tablespoon vanilla extract
2	pints fresh berries
	Fresh mint leaves for garnish

- **Mix cheese, honey and vanilla in food processor until smooth.**

- **Spoon into individual stemmed glasses and top with fresh fruit.**

SERVING SUGGESTIONS:

Drizzle with melted chocolate.

Garnish with fresh mint leaf.

Can be layered in a sundae type dish or trifle bowl.

Stress Free
Soups, Salads & Dressings

Italian Fish Soup

I had a soup in Bermuda that was so wonderful, I had to come home and try to recreate it. Since I am Italian, I call it Italian Fish Soup.

Serves 6 to 8   Equipment: 8 quart soup pot

	Olive oil
1	cup onion, chopped
1	cup celery, chopped
1	cup carrot, sliced
2	cups Yukon gold potatoes, unpeeled and diced
3	cloves garlic, minced
1	cup fresh basil, chopped
½	cup fresh oregano, roughly chopped
	Fine sea salt
	Freshly ground pepper
28	ounces canned diced tomatoes
1	green bell pepper, diced
¼	cup Worcestershire sauce
1	pound thick white fillet such as cod
48	ounces fish stock
	Dry sherry

- Place enough olive oil in the bottom of your soup pot just to cover. Add the onion, celery, carrot and potato. Cook on medium heat 5 minutes, stirring occasionally to prevent sticking.

- Add garlic, basil, oregano, salt and pepper. Give a quick stir to heat and release aromas of herbs. Cook 1 minute.

- Add tomatoes, bell pepper, Worcestershire, fish and fish stock. Simmer 10 to 15 minutes. Season with salt and pepper.

- Soup can be finished with a splash of sherry which guests can add themselves.

COOK'S TIPS:

Frozen fish fillets can be kept on hand to make this soup on a moment's notice.

Tortellini Soup with Sun-Dried Tomato, Baby Spinach and Fresh Cremini Mushrooms

Make this soup on a moment's notice from your pantry and freezer. It can be on the table in 30 minutes or less, and can be served as an entrée or an appetizer.

Serves 6 to 8   Equipment: 8 quart soup pot with lid, grater

	Extra virgin olive oil
2	cloves garlic, minced
32	ounces chicken stock
32	ounces vegetable stock
28	ounces diced tomatoes
4	ounces chopped sun-dried tomatoes (not in oil)
12	ounces water
1	cup fresh basil, chopped
½	cup fresh oregano, roughly chopped
2	cups baby spinach
10	ounces frozen cheese tortellini
10	ounces sliced fresh cremini mushrooms
	Parmigiano-Reggiano

- Heat olive oil and garlic in soup pot over medium heat until garlic is fragrant.

- Add stocks, both types of tomatoes and 12 ounces of water. Bring to boil.

- Add basil, oregano, spinach, tortellini and mushrooms and cook until tortellini are done, approximately 10 minutes. More water or stock can be added to achieve desired consistency.

- Sprinkle with freshly grated Parmigiano-Reggiano.

Cook's Tips:

The sun-dried tomatoes do not have to be rehydrated since we are adding them to hot liquid.

63

Minestrone Soup
(Italian Vegetable, Bean and Pasta Soup)

Minestrone means big soup in Italian. It is usually a soup that is considered a whole meal. This soup is also a great comfort food to bring to friends and neighbors in times of need.

Serves 8 to 10   Equipment: 8 to 10 quart soup pot

	Olive oil
2	cups chopped onion
6-8	cloves garlic, minced
1½	cups sliced celery
1½	cups sliced carrots
2	cups quartered and thinly sliced zucchini
2	cups peeled and diced eggplant
56	ounces canned diced tomatoes
4	cups chicken or vegetable stock
6	cups water
2	canned small white beans or chickpeas, drained and rinsed well
1½	cups uncooked small pasta, such as ditalini or acini di pepe
1	cup fresh basil, roughly chopped
½	cup fresh oregano, finely chopped
4	bay leaves
1	teaspoon fine sea salt
	Freshly ground pepper, to taste
	Parmigiano-Reggiano, grated

- Thinly film the soup pot with olive oil. Add onion and cook until it begins to brown. Add garlic, celery and carrots. Sauté 3 to 5 minutes but do not let garlic get to the dark brown or black stage.

- Add zucchini, eggplant, tomatoes, stock, water and beans. Cook until vegetables are tender, 10 to 15 minutes.

- Add pasta, herbs, salt and a few grindings of pepper. Cook until pasta is al dente, approximately 15 to 20 minutes.

Minestrone Soup continued

SERVING SUGGESTION:

Serve with a sprinkle of freshly grated Parmigiano-Reggiano,
a mixed green salad and crusty bread for a satisfying meal.

COOK'S TIPS:

Remove the bay leaves before serving. They are sharp and can cause injury if swallowed.

Since this is such a "big" soup, you might find that
you want to add more water to achieve desired consistency.

Rinsing the beans also eliminates any gasses that
are sometimes unpleasant. The bubbles that you
see when you open the can are from the gas.

Cream of Potato Soup

Serves 4 to 6 as first course

3   pounds Yukon gold potatoes, peeled and cut into 1-inch chunks

3   cups chicken or vegetable stock

3   whole garlic cloves

2   bay leaves

Fine sea salt

Freshly ground pepper

- Cook potatoes, garlic, salt, a few grinds of black pepper and bay leaves in chicken stock until potatoes are fork tender, approximately 20 minutes.

- Remove bay leaves.

- Place in food processor and pulse until smooth.

- Adjust salt and pepper to taste.

Vegetable Soup

Serves 6 to 8   Equipment: soup pot with lid

Olive oil

3   large carrots, halved lengthwise
     and sliced

3   celery ribs, sliced

1   cup chopped onion

1   large zucchini, quartered and sliced

1   large yellow squash, quartered and
     sliced

10   ounces fresh mushrooms, sliced

1   red bell pepper, diced

1   head broccoli, cut into florets

4   cups stock of your choice,
     vegetable, chicken, or mushroom

¼   cup fresh basil, chopped

2   tablespoons fresh oregano, chopped

     Fine sea salt

     Freshly ground pepper

     Additional chicken or vegetable
     stock, if necessary

     Additional herbs for garnish

- Pour enough olive oil in soup pot to just cover bottom. Heat to medium.

- Add carrots, celery, and onion and cook 5 to 10 minutes until softened.

- Add zucchini, yellow squash, mushrooms, red bell pepper, broccoli and stock. Cook another 20 minutes.

- Add more stock if you want a thinner consistency. Add basil and oregano. Season with salt and pepper to taste. Add more stock if soup is too thick.

- Cook 5 minutes.

- Serve with additional fresh herbs as garnish.

COOK'S TIP:

Soup can be pureed in a food processor
for a "cream of vegetable" soup.

White Bean Soup

This soup was inspired by our trip to Italy. We ate White Bean Soup all over Tuscany and loved it all.

Serves 6 to 8   Equipment: 8 quart soup pot, grater

	Extra virgin olive oil
2	cups diced onion
4	large garlic cloves, minced
1	cup carrot, ½-inch thick slices
1	cup celery, ½-inch thick slices
2	teaspoons dried marjoram (or oregano)
2	teaspoons dried basil
4	cups dry, small white beans, which have been soaked overnight, or 3 (15 to 16 ounce) cans, drained and rinsed well
2-2½	quarts chicken stock
2	bay leaves
1	teaspoon fine sea salt
4-5	turns of freshly ground pepper
8	cups chopped Tuscan kale or baby spinach
	Parmigiano-Reggiano for garnish

- **Thinly film the soup pot with oil. Add onion and cook until browned. Add garlic, carrots, and celery. Cook until celery begins to soften, approximately 2 to 3 minutes. Pinch marjoram and basil between your fingers and rub to release oils. Let herbs fall into soup. Mix well and cook 2 minutes to release flavors of the herbs.**

- **Add beans, stock, and bay leaves. Season with salt and pepper. Cook at least 1 hour. Add chopped kale and cook another 20 to 30 minutes until kale is tender.**

COOK'S TIPS:

This soup will thicken if allowed to cook several hours.
It can be made a day or two ahead which will also help it thicken.
Prior to the addition of the kale, a small portion of the soup
can be placed in the food processor or blender
for a thicker consistency.
When making soup with dried beans,
it will take longer for the soup to thicken.

Apple Poppy Seed Dressing

This low-fat dressing was featured on one of the morning shows so many years ago that I cannot remember where I got it.

Equipment: large bowl or pitcher with tight fitting lid

12	ounces frozen apple juice concentrate, defrosted
9	tablespoons fresh lemon juice
9	tablespoons apple cider vinegar
6	tablespoons Dijon mustard
2	tablespoons canola oil
1½	teaspoons freshly ground pepper
1½	teaspoons poppy seeds

• **Mix all ingredients together. Keep in a tightly covered container.**

SERVING SUGGESTION:

Great over baby spinach with walnuts and Mandarin oranges.

Tre Colore Salad with Orange Vinaigrette, Gorgonzola and Pignoli Nuts

Something so beautiful and tasty you will want it with every meal.

Equipment: large salad bowl, salad spinner (optional)

1	head green leaf lettuce
1	small head radicchio
1	medium head Belgian endive
¼	cup crumbled Gorgonzola cheese
¼	cup pignoli nuts, toasted
1	recipe Vinaigrette (in Basics chapter p. 16) with 1 drop orange oil added

- **Wash and dry salad ingredients. Place in large salad bowl.**

- **Top with crumbled Gorgonzola cheese and toasted pignoli nuts.**

- **Add dressing in small amounts and toss well.**

VARIATIONS:

Use a variety of greens or baby spinach
Select cheeses and nuts that complement the rest of the meal.

COOK'S TIPS:

Salad should not be swimming in dressing. It's better to add less and decide you need more.
Drying the greens in a salad spinner helps the dressing cling to the greens.
Pignoli nuts are also known as pine nuts.

SERVING SUGGESTION:

Serve with Easy Cheese Soufflé found on p. 129.

Black-Eyed Peas and Orange Salad

Also known as cowpeas, black-eyed peas are rich in fiber, potassium, protein and iron, but low in fat and sodium.

Equipment: 10 to 12-inch sauté pan

	Canola oil
2	cloves garlic, minced
1	cup shredded red cabbage
4	cups baby spinach
15	ounces canned black-eyed peas, drained
2	navel oranges, peeled, halved and sliced ¼-inch thick
	Raspberry vinegar
1	medium sweet onion, shaved
½	cup walnuts, chopped

- Thinly film a large sauté pan with canola oil and heat to medium.

- Add garlic and cabbage and sauté until cabbage begins to wilt. Add spinach and wilt slightly.

- Divide spinach and cabbage between 4 dinner plates. Top with a spoon of black-eyed peas and slices of ½ an orange.

- Drizzle with raspberry vinegar. Sprinkle shaved onion and walnuts on top.

Grilled Escarole with Toasted Garlic, White Beans and Lemon Thyme Vinaigrette

This beautiful salad can be made ahead and kept at room temperature until serving time. The toasted garlic is a taste treat and great on other dishes as well.

Serves 4

Equipment: grill or sauté pan, pastry brush, 4 beautiful salad plates or large platter, slotted spoon, small saucepan

1	head escarole cut lengthwise in quarters through core, so the leaves stay intact
¼	cup olive oil, plus extra for brushing on greens
8	large cloves garlic, sliced lengthwise
1	lemon, juiced
8	sprigs fresh thyme
15	ounces canned small white beans, drained and rinsed well
	Fine sea salt
	Freshly ground pepper
	Lemon slices for garnish

- **Wash and dry escarole. Lightly brush with olive oil. Grill or sauté until lightly browned and only slightly wilted. Can be done ahead. Place on platter or individual salad plates and hold at room temperature.**

- **Place ¼ cup olive oil in small saucepan. Heat and then add sliced garlic. Watch carefully and cook until golden. Remove garlic from oil with slotted spoon.**

- **Mix the warm olive oil with lemon juice, thyme and beans. Add salt and pepper to taste. Set aside. This step can be done several hours ahead.**

- **Place 1 piece of escarole on each plate. Divide beans and dressing among the four plates and sprinkle with toasted garlic. Garnish with lemon slice and serve at room temperature.**

SERVING SUGGESTION:

Can be served with grilled chicken for a complete meal.

COOK'S TIP:

Escarole can be very sandy, so it must be carefully washed. Fill your sink with water, swish the lettuce in the water to release dirt. Let the dirt fall to the bottom of the sink and lift lettuce out without stirring the water.

Couscous Salad

Large grain couscous is a taste treat but takes longer to cook than regular couscous.

Serves 6 to 8   Equipment: garlic peeler, baking sheet, parchment paper, ovenproof baking dish

2	cups couscous, large preferred, but small will work
4-5	cups chicken or vegetable broth
3	very small zucchini, cut into 1-inch pieces
8	cloves garlic, peeled but whole
1	cup largely chopped eggplant, (approximately 1-inch pieces)
2	medium onions, cut into ⅛
3	plum tomatoes chopped
1	tablespoon fresh oregano, chopped
1	tablespoon fresh basil, chiffonade
¼	cup balsamic vinegar
½	cup olive oil, divided ¼ cup and ¼ cup
	Fresh Italian parsley, chopped

- Cook couscous according to package directions, using broth instead of water.

- Place vegetables (except tomatoes) and garlic on baking sheet lined with parchment so that they are in one single layer. Drizzle with ¼ cup olive oil. Roast in 400 degree oven for 20 minutes or until tender. Cool. Add tomatoes when vegetables are cooled. Add herbs.

- Mix couscous and vegetables. Slowly whisk together ¼ cup oil into vinegar; add to couscous. Mix well.

- Place on large platter. Serve immediately.

SERVING SUGGESTION:

Garnish with fresh herbs, chopped tomatoes, or sliced oranges.

COOK'S TIP:

Great for picnics, make ahead meals or brown bag lunches.

Purple Potato Salad with Green Beans and Tear Drop Tomatoes

This salad brings color and variety to your table.

Serves 6 to 8   Equipment: whisk, mixing bowl, serving bowl, vegetable steamer

---

3	pounds purple potatoes
1	pint red teardrop, cherry or grape tomatoes
1	pound green beans, stemmed
¼	cup red wine vinegar
1	teaspoon Dijon mustard
	Fine sea salt
	Freshly ground pepper
½	cup extra virgin olive oil
½	cup fresh basil, torn at last minute

- Cut potatoes into bite-size pieces and boil until tender. Drain well.

- Wash and dry tomatoes. Cut in half, if desired.

- Steam green beans 6 to 8 minutes.

- Place vinegar, mustard, salt and pepper bowl. Slowly whisk in olive oil until combined well.

- Place potatoes and green beans in a large bowl and toss with dressing. Add tomatoes and basil.

- Serve at room temperature.

COOK'S TIP:

If purple potatoes are not readily available, you can substitute Yukon Gold or Red Bliss.

Wild Rice & Chicken Salad

This is a great summer main dish salad.

Serves 4 to 6

1	pound boneless skinless chicken breast, poached, cooled and diced (see recipe for Poached Chicken Breast, p. 22)
2	cups wild rice, cooked
1	cup seedless red and green grapes
½	cup champagne vinegar
¼	cup chopped fresh thyme, plus additional for garnish
½	cup extra virgin olive oil, have extra available if desired
	Fine sea salt
	Freshly ground pepper to taste
4-6	cups baby greens

- Cook wild rice according to package; this will take approximately 45 to 60 minutes.

- If grapes are large they can be sliced in half.

- Mix champagne vinegar and thyme. Slowly whisk in ½ cup olive oil. Season with salt and pepper. Add more oil if dressing tastes too acidic.

- Combine chicken, rice and grapes. Season to taste with salt and pepper. Add dressing to taste. Serve over baby greens with additional thyme as garnish.

Stress Free…

Notes

Stress Free
Pasta
& Risotto

Create a Pasta

Have fun creating your own signature dish.

Equipment: 10 to 12-inch sauté pan, cheese grater, 8 quart soup pot

1	pound pasta (shape of your choice)
	Extra virgin olive oil
3	garlic cloves, minced
3	cups fresh vegetables, cut into bite-size pieces, such as broccoli, red bell pepper, zucchini, onion, carrots, green beans, eggplant, peas
½	cup fresh basil leaves, chiffonade or 2 tablespoons dried basil
½	cup fresh Italian parsley, chopped, or 2 tablespoons dried parsley
¼	cup fresh oregano, chopped, or 1 tablespoon dried oregano
2¼	cups chicken or vegetable stock, divided ¼ cup and 2 cups
	Balsamic vinegar
	Additional chopped fresh herbs for garnish
½	cup freshly grated Parmigiano-Reggiano
1	cup dry white wine
	Optional: Large frozen shrimp, peeled and deveined, see Cook's Tip.

- Cook pasta in 8 quarts of boiling salted water. Drain and set aside.

- Heat your sauté pan and thinly film with oil. Add garlic and cook until fragrant. Do not brown.

- Add fresh vegetables and approximately ¼ cup stock and sauté until crisp and tender.

- Sprinkle with balsamic vinegar and garnish with fresh herbs and Parmigiano-Reggiano cheese.

- Add remaining stock and wine and bring to a boil. Immediately turn down to low. Add pasta and herbs and toss well.

COOK'S TIP:

You can add large uncooked frozen shrimp, during the last step, once you have turned pan to low. Cover the pan and steam 3 to 5 minutes until shrimp are pink.

Sautéed Angel Hair Pasta Nests with Tomato, Basil & White Wine

This no boil pasta dish always gets rave reviews!

Serves 4   Equipment: 8 to 10-inch sauté pan with lid

4-8	angel hair pasta nests, (also called fidellini or fideos) or pasta, enough for 4 portions - see Cook's Tip for quantity
	Olive oil
2	garlic cloves, minced
1	cup fresh basil leaves, chiffonade
¼	cup fresh oregano leaves, chopped
1	teaspoon fine sea salt
	Freshly ground black pepper to taste
28	ounces canned diced tomatoes
1	cup dry white wine or chicken or vegetable stock
	Parmigiano-Reggiano for garnish

- Thinly film a sauté pan with olive oil. Heat and add pasta nests. Brown pasta on each side.

- Add garlic, basil and oregano in between nests and cook until fragrant.

- Season with salt and pepper.

- Add tomatoes and wine or stock. Liquid should cover pasta. Cover and cook 10 minutes to cook pasta.

- Garnish with a sprinkle of Parmigiano-Reggiano and additional chopped fresh herbs.

COOK'S TIPS:

The pasta nests come in many sizes so you have to use your judgment in determining how many to use. A good guideline is to use enough to comfortably fill the pan without crowding. One pound of fresh, peeled, deveined shrimp can be added during last 3 to 5 minutes of cooking time. A nonstick pan is not recommended, as it does not conduct heat efficiently enough for this dish.

Pasta with White Clam Sauce

Why go out when you can create this at home. Don't forget the candles and Pinot Grigio or Vernaccia!

Serves 4   Equipment: 10 to 12-inch sauté pan with lid

	Olive oil
4	fettuccine or tagliatelle pasta nests or pasta enough for 4 portions - see Cook's Tip for quantity
2	cloves garlic, minced
1	cup fresh basil leaves, chopped, plus additional for garnish
¼	cup fresh oregano leaves, chopped, plus additional for garnish
¼	cup Italian parsley, chopped, plus additional for garnish
1½	cups dry white wine or clam juice
2	(10-ounce) cans baby clams
3	cups water
2	cups chicken stock
¼	cup freshly squeezed lemon juice
1	teaspoon fine sea salt
	Freshly ground pepper, to taste
	Parmigiano-Reggiano

- Thinly film sauté pan with olive oil. Heat to medium and add pasta nests. Brown pasta on each side.

- Add garlic and herbs in between nests and cook until fragrant.

- Add wine or clam juice, canned clams, water, stock, lemon juice, salt and pepper. Liquid should cover pasta. Cover and cook 10 minutes to cook pasta. At this point, pasta nests can be tossed to separate.

- Sprinkle with Parmigiano-Reggiano and additional chopped fresh herbs.

COOK'S TIPS:

Littleneck clams can be added near the end of the cooking time for an added treat. Add clams, cover and cook until clams open.

The pasta nests come in many sizes so you have to use your judgment in determining how many to use. A good guideline is to use enough to comfortably fill the pan without crowding.

Angel hair pasta nests would also work if fettuccine or tagliatelle are not available.

Bow Tie Pasta Bathed in Morel Cream Sauce

The nooks and crannies in a morel are good hiding places for sauce.

Serves 4 to 6   Equipment: 10 to 12-inch sauté pan, grater

1	pound bow tie pasta
	Olive oil
1	shallot, finely minced
2	garlic cloves, chopped
4	ounces dried morels, rehydrated
½	cup chicken or vegetable stock
½	cup light cream
	Fine sea salt
	Freshly ground pepper
½	cup Italian parsley, chopped
	Parmigiano-Reggiano for grating

- Cook pasta to al dente stage. Set aside.

- Thinly film sauté pan with olive oil. Heat and add shallot and garlic. Cook 3 to 5 minutes.

- Add morels, stock and cream and simmer 15 minutes.

- Season with salt and pepper to taste. Add parsley.

- Toss with pasta and sprinkle with Parmigiano-Reggiano.

COOK'S TIP:

To rehydrate dried items, bring a small pot of water to a boil.
Remove from heat and place dried ingredient in pan for 3 to 5 minutes or until soft.
Save liquid for sauces or soups.

Fresh Tomato and Basil Sauce

No cooking required for this sauce.

Yield: Enough for ½ pound pasta

12	plum tomatoes, chopped
2	cloves garlic, chopped
1	shallot, minced
	Extra virgin olive oil
	Freshly ground pepper
½	teaspoon fine sea salt
1	cup fresh basil leaves

- Mix tomatoes, garlic, and shallot. Add olive oil, salt and pepper.

- Tear basil leaves and add to tomato mixture.

- Toss with cooked pasta.

Variation:

Add chunks of fresh mozzarella.

Can also be used as a topping for bruschetta.

Cook's Tip:

Cook the whole pound of pasta and save half for another meal.

Place unsauced pasta in a large plastic bag in the refrigerator for up to 5 days.

Orzo Pilaf

Serves 4   Equipment: 10 to 12-inch sauté pan

Olive oil

1   cup uncooked orzo
     (rice shaped pasta)

2   shallots, minced

1   clove garlic, minced

2-3 cups chicken or vegetable stock

¼   cup finely minced Italian parsley

Fine sea salt

Freshly ground black pepper

- Place just enough olive oil in pan to lightly coat bottom. Heat oil.

- Add orzo and cook until grains begin to turn golden brown.

- Add shallot and garlic. Toss well and cook 1 to 2 minutes.

- Add 2 cups stock and cook on medium until absorbed. Add more stock slowly until orzo is cooked, approximately 10 minutes.

- Add parsley, salt and pepper to taste.

COOK'S TIP:

Orzo is a rice shaped pasta that is also called Riso. It can vary
in shape from short and fat to long and narrow. The shape variation will also
affect the cooking time, so use 10 minutes as a guideline along with
your good judgment to determine doneness.

Pasta with Diced Tomato and Zucchini

Equipment: 10 to 12-inch sauté pan, large pot for pasta

1	pound spaghetti, penne or rotini
	Olive oil
2	cloves garlic, minced
2	medium zucchini, quartered and sliced ¼-inch thick
6-8	large ripe plum tomatoes
	Fine sea salt
	Freshly ground pepper
1	cup chicken or vegetable stock
1	cup fresh basil, chopped
½	cup grated Parmigiano-Reggiano

- Cook pasta to al dente stage, approximately 8 to 10 minutes. While pasta is cooking, start the sauce.

- Thinly film a sauté pan with olive oil. Add garlic and cook until fragrant. Add zucchini. Sauté until tender and crisp. Add tomatoes and toss with zucchini.

- Season with sea salt and pepper.

- Add enough stock to make a sauce consistency. Add basil and toss.

- Pour over pasta. Toss gently. Sprinkle with Parmigiano-Reggiano.

Pasta with Broccoli and Parmigiano-Reggiano

Serves 4 to 6   Equipment: vegetable steamer, 10 to 12-inch sauté pan, cheese grater

1	pound penne or ziti pasta
1	head broccoli or broccolini
4	cloves garlic, minced
	Olive oil
	Chicken or vegetable stock, approximately 1 cup
	White wine or vermouth, approximately ½ cup
	Fine sea salt
	Freshly ground pepper
	Parmigiano-Reggiano

- Cook pasta according to package directions.

- Steam whole broccoli (or broccolini) until crisp and tender. Cut into florets after steaming to save nutrients. (Save steaming water if desired.)

- Sauté garlic in olive oil until soft. Add pasta and broccoli along with stock, white wine or broccoli steaming water. Season to taste with salt and pepper.

- Heat thoroughly and cook gently 3 to 5 minutes to allow flavors to blend.

- When serving, pass Parmigiano-Reggiano and grater so that diners can add to taste.

COOK'S TIP:

You can save the cooking water from steamed vegetables to use in future sauces or soups for added nutrients.

Penne with Chicken and Wild Mushrooms

Serves 6 to 8   Equipment: cheese grater 10 to 12-inch sauté pan

4	chicken cutlets, cut into bite-size pieces
1	pound penne pasta
	Olive oil
2	garlic cloves, chopped
1½	pounds mixed mushrooms, roughly chopped
½	cup fresh basil, chopped
¼	cup Italian parsley, chopped
½	cup vegetable stock
½	cup dry white wine or dry vermouth
	Fine sea salt
	Freshly ground pepper
	Parmigiano-Reggiano (chunk)

- Trim chicken and cut into bite-size pieces. Set aside in your refrigerator.

- Cook penne to al dente stage. While penne is cooking, start chicken and mushroom sauce.

- Heat sauté pan and add enough olive oil to thinly coat the bottom of the pan.

- Add garlic and chicken and cook 2 to 3 minutes. Add mushrooms. Cook 3 to 5 minutes.

- Add herbs, stock and wine. Bring to boil and immediately turn to low. Season with salt and pepper to taste. Add pasta and toss well.

- Grate Parmigiano-Reggiano to garnish.

COOK'S TIP:

Pasta should be cooked al dente, an Italian phrase meaning "to the tooth."
It will yield slightly when bitten into.

Shrimp, White Bean and Broccoli Sauce

Great with a loaf of Tuscan bread and a green salad!

Yield: enough for 1 pound of pasta	Equipment: cheese grater, sauté pan with lid

	Extra virgin olive oil
1	head broccoli, cut into florets
½	cup chicken stock
1	pound large shrimp, peeled and deveined
2	cloves garlic, minced
2	cups small white beans, drained and rinsed
	Fine sea salt
	Freshly ground pepper, to taste
1	pound cooked pasta
	Parmigiano-Reggiano

- Thinly film the sauté pan with extra virgin olive oil. Add broccoli and chicken stock. Cover and cook 5 minutes.

- Add large shrimp. Toss well and cover. Add garlic and white beans and cook until shrimp are pink.

- Add salt and pepper to taste. Toss well and serve over your favorite pasta.

- Pass the cheese grater and the Parmigiano-Reggiano.

Macaroni and Cheese

Show the kids the real thing! It's simple to do and freezes well.

Equipment: pasta pot, 4 quart saucepan, 9-inch square casserole dish

½	pound pasta (shape of your choice)
2	tablespoons unsalted butter
¼	cup flour
2½	cups 1% milk
6	ounces shredded Cheddar cheese (2%) fat, reserving ¼ cup for topping
	Fine sea salt
	Freshly ground pepper

- Cook pasta to al dente stage. Drain and set aside.

- Preheat oven to 375 degrees.

- In a 4 quart saucepan, melt butter and whisk in flour. The mixture will be dry. Cook 2 minutes and add half the milk. Whisk until smooth. Add remaining milk and whisk again until smooth. Cook until thickened, approximately 3 to 5 minutes.

- Remove pan from heat. Gradually add cheese ¼ cup at a time, whisking until smooth. Season with salt and pepper.

- Mix cheese sauce with pasta and place in 9-inch square casserole dish. Top with additional grated cheese.

- Bake at 375 degrees until casserole bubbles and cheese topping is melted.

COOK'S TIPS:

Remember to cook pasta in at least 4 to 6 quarts of water.
Cooking pasta in too small a pot or too little water will result in sticky, gummy pasta.
Using a larger pot than you think you will need is a good idea.
Mix chopped fresh herbs such as parsley and chives into the cheese sauce.
Add ¼ cup bread crumbs to the cheese topping before sprinkling on top.

Risotto with Porcini Mushrooms

The key to good risotto is the slow absorption of the hot liquid, which takes 20 to 40 minutes.

Serves 4 as main course, 6 to 8 as first course

Equipment: chef's pan or 5 quart saucepan, 4 quart saucepan, coffee filter placed inside strainer, strainer placed over a bowl

1½	cups dry white wine
4	cups stock, such as chicken or mushroom
1	cup dried porcini, rehydrated
	Extra virgin olive oil
1	cup onion, chopped
2	cups Carnaroli or Arborio rice, checked over for imperfect grains
½	teaspoon fine sea salt
½	teaspoon freshly ground pepper
½	cup freshly grated Parmigiano-Reggiano
2	tablespoons finely minced Italian parsley

- To rehydrate the mushrooms: in a 4 quart saucepan, bring wine and stock to a boil and keep simmering on stove. Add porcini and simmer 5 minutes. Drain this mixture through the coffee filter and reserve liquid. Reserve porcini and chop into bite-size pieces. Place stock/wine back in pan and simmer. (The purpose of straining is to clear the liquid of any dirt that might have been on the porcini.)

- Using a heavy 5 quart saucepan or chef's pan, thinly film the pan with olive oil and add onion. Sauté until onion starts to soften. Add rice, salt and pepper and coat rice grains with olive oil mixture. Add stock mixture 1 cup at a time and stir until each addition of liquid is absorbed. This takes time and patience. After last addition of stock is absorbed, add Parmigiano-Reggiano. When all of the stock is absorbed, which can take anywhere from 20 to 40 minutes, and rice grains are creamy, you can add the parsley and porcini.

VARIATION:

Add sautéed chicken, which has been cut into bite-size pieces along with the porcini.

COOK'S TIP:

Risotto must be served immediately. It does not wait!

Notes

Stress Free
Entrées

Arctic Char Poached with White Wine, Lemon and Rosemary

Arctic char is a wonderfully sweet, pink fleshed fish that is a cousin to salmon and trout. It is slightly larger than a trout and sweeter than salmon. This fish is exceptionally pleasing to those who find salmon a bit strong.

Serves 2   Equipment: 10 to 12-inch sauté pan with lid

2	cups dry white wine such as Sauvignon Blanc or Pinot Grigio (or stock)
4	sprigs fresh rosemary
½	teaspoon fine sea salt
	Freshly ground pepper
2	fresh lemons, sliced thinly
1	pound arctic char fillet, skin removed
	Additional rosemary for garnish

- **Prepare pan for poaching fish: Place wine or stock, 4 sprigs rosemary, salt, a few grinds of black pepper, and slices of one lemon in sauté pan.**

- **Add fish, bring to low boil, cover and simmer until fish is done, approximately 10 minutes.**

- **Serve with additional lemon slices and sprigs of rosemary.**

COOK'S TIP:

You can ask your seafood manager
to remove the skin from the fish for you.

Grilled Sea Bass with Mediterranean Vegetables

A piquant marinade combined with a simple cooking method results in a complex taste sensation.

Serves 2 to 3   Equipment: grill, large shallow baking dish

Marinade for sea bass and vegetables:

2	tablespoons capers
2	tablespoons olive oil
2	tablespoons black olive paste or ⅓ cup finely chopped black olives
2	tablespoons balsamic vinegar
2	tablespoons fresh lemon juice
½	cup fresh oregano

1	pound Chilean sea bass
1	fennel bulb, sliced
1	small eggplant, sliced into ½-inch thick rounds
1	small zucchini, sliced ½-inch thick lengthwise
2	red bell peppers, sliced into rounds and seeded
1	large onion, sliced ¼-inch thick
2	lemons, sliced and reserved for garnish

- Mix all marinade ingredients together.

- Marinate sea bass and vegetables 20 to 30 minutes in large shallow baking dish.

- Heat grill or broiler until very hot.

- Place sea bass and vegetables directly on hot grill or on baking sheet if using broiler. Grill with lid down (roast) 10 minutes on each side.

- Plate in decorative fashion with fresh herbs and lemon slices for garnish

---

COOK'S TIP:

A large grill pan can also be used in place of outdoor grill.

Salmon with Black Bean and Mango Salsa

This dish is so beautiful you will want to make it again and again. The contrast of colors is exquisite and it takes very little time to prepare.

Serves 2 to 3   Equipment: Grill or grill pan or 10 to 12-inch sauté pan

---

| 1 | pound thick salmon fillet, skinless, cut into 4 to 6 ounce pieces |

Salmon Marinade:

1	tablespoon honey
2	teaspoons soy sauce
1	tablespoon olive oil
	Fine sea salt
	Freshly ground pepper

Black Bean Salsa:

15	ounces black beans, drained and rinsed
1	soft mango, diced
½	teaspoon ground cumin
1	tablespoon olive oil
½	cup chopped cilantro
2	fresh limes, juiced, divided
2	tablespoons minced red onion
⅛	teaspoon fine sea salt
	Few grinds freshly ground pepper

- Prepare marinade: mix honey, soy sauce, olive oil, pinch sea salt and a few grinds of pepper together for salmon marinade. Place salmon in marinade for at least 20 minutes and up to 2 hours.

- Mix together remaining ingredients to make black bean salsa. Prepare the salsa early in the day, if possible, to allow flavors to blend.

- To cook salmon: heat grill, grill pan or sauté pan. Add salmon and sear on all sides until nicely browned.

- To plate: place a large spoon of salsa on plate and place salmon on top. Garnish with fresh cilantro sprigs.

Salmon with Black Bean and Mango Salsa continued

VARIATIONS:

Mango Kiwi Relish

1	mango, diced
2	kiwis, peeled and diced
¼	cup cilantro, roughly chopped
1	orange, juiced

• **Mix all ingredients together and serve with pan seared salmon. If you can make the relish while you are marinating the fish it will give these flavors a chance to blend as well.**

Strawberry Kiwi Relish

1	cup strawberries, diced
2	kiwis, peeled and diced
¼	cup cilantro, roughly chopped
1	orange, juiced

• **Mix all ingredients together and serve with pan seared salmon. If you can make the relish while you are marinating the fish, it will give these flavors a chance to blend as well.**

COOK'S TIPS:

Remember to buy your mango a little on the
soft side so that you can use it within a few days.
The Black Bean Salsa, Mango Kiwi and Strawberry Kiwi Relishes
are also nice with any grilled protein.

Asian Stuffed Salmon Fillet

This dish can also be cooked on your grill.

Serves 4 to 6   Equipment: sauté pan, baking dish, heavy duty aluminum foil

---

Peanut oil

3	baby bok choy, thinly sliced vertically
6	ounce bag baby spinach
2	cups or ½ pound fresh bean sprouts
10	ounces fresh mushrooms, sliced
2	carrots, shredded
3	scallions, sliced thinly
2	inches ginger, peeled and grated or finely minced
2	cloves garlic, minced
¼	cup light soy sauce
2	pounds salmon fillet, as thick as possible
½	cup honey
¼	cup Dijon mustard

- Pour enough peanut oil in sauté pan to barely cover bottom. Add all vegetables, ginger and garlic.

- Cook until tender but firm. Add soy sauce. Cook 5 minutes more.

- Cut salmon through center lengthwise and stuff with vegetables.

- Mix honey and mustard. Brush fish with honey mustard.

- Wrap fish in foil. Grill or bake in very hot oven, 450 degrees, until fish is flaky, approximately 20-30 minutes.

Snapper with Shallot, Basil, Zucchini and Tomato

Serves 4   Equipment: 10 to 12-inch sauté pan with cover, large plate

1½- 2 pounds snapper fillet,
    (a large thick piece is best)

1   teaspoon fine sea salt
    Freshly ground pepper
    Olive oil

2   shallots, minced

1   clove garlic, minced

4   small zucchini, about 4 to 6 inches
    long, sliced into ¼-inch rounds

¾   cup dry white wine such as Pinot
    Grigio or Sauvignon Blanc, or
    chicken or fish stock

4   very ripe plum tomatoes, chopped

½   cup fresh basil, chopped or
    chiffonade - see Glossary

- Season fish with salt and pepper and refrigerate.

- Heat sauté pan and lightly film with olive oil

- Sauté shallot and garlic until shallot starts to become translucent.

- Add zucchini and sauté 1 to 2 minutes. Remove from pan.

- Add snapper and sauté on each side. Add white wine or stock. Cover and simmer until fish is done. This will vary depending on the thickness of your fish, use 10 minutes per inch of thickness as a guideline.

- Return zucchini mixture to pan and add the chopped tomatoes and fresh basil. Heat thoroughly.

SERVING SUGGESTION:

Serve with pasta, rice, couscous or crusty Italian bread.

Stir-Fried Shrimp with Seasonal Vegetables

Serves 4   Equipment: 10 to 12-inch sauté pan, chef's pan or wok

1	pound large shrimp, peeled and deveined
1	cup white wine
1	tablespoon fish sauce
1	tablespoon cornstarch
1	cup fish stock
2	tablespoons peanut oil
2-3	cloves garlic, peeled and sliced
1	inch piece ginger, peeled and sliced
3	cups seasonal vegetables or your favorite vegetables, cut into bite-size pieces (keeping in mind that longer cooking vegetables should be cut into smaller pieces)
2	cups cooked jasmine rice

- Marinate shrimp in white wine and fish sauce.

- Mix 1 tablespoon of cornstarch with 1 cup stock.

- Heat oil in a large sauté pan, chef's pan or wok.

- Add garlic and ginger and cook until golden. Remove.

- Add longer cooking vegetables first and work down to quicker cooking items.

- Push vegetables to the side of the pan. Drain shrimp and reserve marinade. Add shrimp to pan and cook until pink.

- Mix reserved marinade with cornstarch mixture and add to stir-fry. Cook until sauce is thickened and serve over jasmine rice.

COOK'S TIP:

See Stir-Fry Guidelines on p.29.

Swordfish with Horseradish Crust

For something a little different or for those who are not fond of fish, this recipe is the one to try. Your taste buds will focus on the horseradish crust allowing you to learn to enjoy a fish meal.

Equipment: food processor with steel blade, 9 x 13-inch baking dish

½	cup prepared horseradish (squeeze dry)
2	scallions, finely chopped
¼	teaspoon wasabi powder
¼	teaspoon ground ginger
¼	teaspoon Dijon mustard
¼	teaspoon lemon zest
½	cup unseasoned bread crumbs
1	teaspoon finely chopped shallot
¼	cup fresh lemon juice
2	tablespoons unsalted butter, at room temperature
4	individual portions of swordfish, approximately 1 pound total weight
½	cup white wine

- **Preheat oven to 475 degrees.**
- **Blend all ingredients (except wine and fish) together in food processor until ball forms. Place fish in baking dish, pat horseradish mixture on top, pour white wine over and bake at 475 degrees for about 20 minutes.**

VARIATION:

This recipe works well with any thick fish steak or even boneless skinless chicken breast.

Chicken with Berry Sauce

This dish is excellent when the strawberries are at their peak!

Serves 4   Equipment: meat pounder, 10 to 12-inch sauté pan

4	boneless, skinless chicken breasts, approximately 3 to 4 ounces each
	Olive oil
1	tablespoon unsalted butter
2	tablespoons champagne vinegar
	Orange oil - 2 to 3 drops (orange extract can be substituted)
2	cups fresh strawberries, sliced, or any combination of your favorite berries
½	cup dried strawberries or cherries
1	cup evaporated skimmed milk, shake well

- Pound chicken breasts to ½-inch thickness.

- Heat sauté pan and thinly film with olive oil. Sauté chicken breast until golden on each side. Remove from pan and place on platter. Cover with foil.

- Add butter to sauté pan. Add vinegar, orange oil and berries. Cook a few minutes to blend flavors.

- Reduce heat to low and add evaporated skimmed milk to bring sauce to desired consistency.

- Place chicken back in sauce and cook 5 minutes, until berries are softened and chicken is done.

Chicken in Red Wine Garlic Sauce with Artichokes and Mushrooms

Add red wine to the sauce for grown-ups or chicken stock for kids.

Serves 4   Equipment: meat pounder, sauté pan

4	boneless, skinless chicken breasts
	Fine sea salt
	Freshly ground pepper to taste
	Olive oil
½	cup fresh basil, chiffonade
1	shallot, minced
10	ounces frozen artichoke hearts, defrosted enough to break apart
10	ounces fresh mushrooms, sliced
½	cup red wine or chicken stock
28	ounces diced canned tomatoes
4	cloves garlic, minced

- Pound chicken to ¼-inch thickness. Season with salt and pepper.
- Heat sauté pan and add olive oil to thinly film bottom of pan.
- Add chicken and sauté until golden on each side.
- Add basil, shallot, artichokes, mushrooms, and red wine (or stock), tomatoes and garlic.
- Cook on low and allow to simmer for 10 minutes.
- Can be served over rice, pasta, or polenta.

Chicken Pot Pie

Comfort food can be enjoyed even if you want to cook healthier.

Serves 4 to 6   Equipment: 9-inch pie plate or equivalent baking dish, 2 saucepans, 4 quarts each

---

	Olive oil
½	cup chopped onion
1	clove garlic, minced
1	cup sliced celery
1	cup carrot, sliced ¼-inch thick
2	tablespoons unsalted butter
¼	cup all-purpose flour
2	cups chicken stock, plus additional, as desired
3	cups Poached Chicken Breast (see recipe p. 22) or leftover chicken
1	cup frozen baby peas
2	tablespoons chopped Italian parsley
1	(9-inch) pie crust, your own or good quality ready-made
	Sea salt
	Freshly ground pepper

- Preheat oven to 375 degrees.

- Heat enough olive oil to thinly film the bottom of the saucepan. Add onion and garlic and cook 2 to 3 minutes until it begins to soften. Add celery and carrot and cook 5 minutes to soften. Set aside.

- Melt butter. Whisk in flour and mix well. Mixture will be dry. Gradually add 1 cup stock to saucepan. Cook 2 to 3 minutes until mixture begins to thicken and takes on a golden color. Add chicken, peas, parsley and additional stock to achieve desired consistency (some like it soupy, some like it thicker). Add salt and pepper to taste.

- Place mixture in baking dish and top with pie crust. Bake at 375 degrees for approximately 25 minutes or until crust is golden and pie is bubbly.

COOK'S TIPS:

Flour mixture must be cooked at least 2 to 3 minutes to lose the uncooked flour taste.

Mashed potatoes can be substituted for the pie crust topping.

Pie can be brushed with butter or olive oil to help crust brown. You can also cut fun shapes out of the pie crust with cookie cutters and place on top of casserole to make it festive.

Pie plate can be sprayed with non-stick cooking spray, Misto or lightly buttered.

Turkey can be used in place of chicken.

Stir-Fried Chicken with Seasonal Vegetables

Get the whole family involved for a fun evening.

Serves 4   Equipment: 10 to 12-   inch sauté pan, chef's pan or wok

---

1	pound boneless, skinless chicken breast, cut into ¼-inch strips
1	cup white wine
1	tablespoon soy sauce
½	cup orange juice
1	tablespoon cornstarch
1	cup chicken stock
2	tablespoons peanut oil
2-3	cloves garlic, peeled and sliced
1	inch piece ginger, peeled and sliced
3	cups seasonal vegetables or your favorite vegetables, cut into bite-size pieces, (keeping in mind that longer cooking vegetables should be cut into smaller pieces)
2	cups cooked jasmine rice

- Marinate chicken in white wine, soy sauce and orange juice.

- Mix 1 tablespoon cornstarch with 1 cup stock.

- Heat oil in sauté pan, chef's pan or wok.

- Add garlic and ginger and cook until golden. Remove.

- Add longer cooking vegetables first and work down to quicker cooking items.

- Push vegetables to the side of the pan. Drain chicken and reserve marinade. Add chicken to pan and cook until opaque.

- Mix reserved marinade with cornstarch mixture and add to stir-fry. Cook until sauce is thickened and serve over jasmine rice.

COOK'S TIP:

Partially frozen chicken slices more thinly.

See Stir-Fry Guidelines on p. 29.

Savory Garlic Chicken

Serves 4   Equipment: 10 to 12-inch sauté pan, meat pounder

4	boneless, skinless chicken breasts
	Fine sea salt
	Freshly ground pepper, to taste
	Olive oil
8	cloves garlic, sliced thinly
1	shallot, minced
6	fresh plum tomatoes, chopped or 15 ounces canned diced tomatoes
½	cup fresh basil, chopped or chiffonade
1	cup white wine or chicken stock

- **Pound chicken to ¼-inch thickness. Season with salt and pepper.**

- **Heat sauté pan and thinly film with olive oil.**

- **Add chicken and sauté 2 to 3 minutes on each side or until golden.**

- **Add garlic, shallot, tomatoes, basil and white wine (or stock).**

- **Cover and cook on low to medium, just below the boil, approximately 10 to 15 minutes.**

SERVING SUGGESTION:

Serve over rice, pasta, or polenta.

COOK'S TIP:

Garlic can either be mashed into the sauce or removed from the dish as desired.

Grilled Chicken with Honey Balsamic Drizzle
The honey adds a bit of sweetness to an average-grade balsamic vinegar.

Equipment: small saucepan, meat pounder, grill pan

1 cup balsamic vinegar
¼ cup mild honey
¼ cup freshly squeezed orange juice
4 pieces boneless, skinless chicken breast
Fine sea salt
Freshly ground pepper

- Place vinegar, honey and orange juice in small saucepan and cook for 15 to 20 minutes, until reduced by half, or to a syrupy consistency.

- Pound chicken breast to even thickness. Season both sides with salt and pepper.

- Heat grill pan. Grill 3 to 4 minutes on each side.

- Drizzle balsamic mixture over grilled chicken.

SERVING SUGGESTION:
Serve over Sautéed Baby Spinach. (see recipe in Basics p. 31)

Enlightened Herb Roast Chicken

Equipment: poultry shears or boning knife, roasting pan, parchment paper

4-5	pound roasting chicken
½	cup fresh basil leaves
¼	cup fresh rosemary
½	cup fresh Italian parsley
5-6	fresh garlic cloves, sliced into rounds
	Olive oil
	Fine sea salt
	Freshly ground mixed peppercorns

- Clean chicken. Cut alongside breastbone separating the chicken into one big flat bird.

- Remove basil, rosemary and parsley from their stems. Mix with garlic slices.

- Gently lift skin and tuck basil, parsley and garlic until skin.

- Lightly brush the outside of the bird with olive oil (or use your oil spray mister). Season with salt and pepper.

- Place skin side up on roasting pan lined with parchment and roast until golden and an internal temperature of 165 degrees, as follows:

  Regular bake - 400 degrees for 1 hour

  Convection bake - 375 degrees for 45 minutes

  Grill on medium/low with lid closed - time will vary depending on grill.

VARIATIONS:

Split Cornish hens, which will cook in 45 minutes.

Individual chicken pieces, which will only take 20 to 30 minutes to cook.

Chicken with Jewel Tone Vegetables

This flash in the pan is as colorful as it is quick, delicious, and nutritious.

Serves 4   Equipment: 10 to 12-inch sauté pan with lid, meat pounder, shallow bowl or pie plate

---

½	cup Wondra flour
½	teaspoon fine sea salt
¼	teaspoon freshly ground pepper
4	pieces boneless, skinless chicken breast
	Olive oil
½	cup white wine
½	cup chicken stock
2	cloves garlic, minced
2	cups baby carrots, sliced lengthwise
1	red bell pepper, sliced into ¼-inch strips
½	pound fresh green beans, stemmed
½	cup flat Italian parsley, roughly chopped, divided ¼ cup and ¼ cup

- Mix flour, salt and pepper in shallow bowl.

- Pound chicken breast to even thickness. Dredge in flour.

- Thinly film sauté pan with olive oil and heat to medium. Add chicken. Brown chicken 3 to 5 minutes on each side until golden. Remove from pan.

- Add the wine and chicken stock to deglaze pan. Add garlic and cook 2 minutes to soften. Return chicken to pan. Add vegetables and ¼ cup parsley. Cover and simmer 5 to 10 minutes, or until vegetables are done to your liking.

- Garnish with remaining parsley.

SERVING SUGGESTION:

Serve over small pasta, rice or couscous.

COOK'S TIP:

Wondra, commonly known as instant flour, is a very fine granular flour
that is also used to make smooth sauces. All-purpose flour can be substituted.

Chicken and Vegetables En Papillote

This is a perfect spa dish you can make at home.

Serves 4   Equipment: parchment paper or heavy duty aluminum foil, large baking sheet

---

24	thin slices of Yukon gold potatoes
4	pieces boneless, skinless chicken breast (approximately 3 to 4 ounces each)
4	cloves garlic, minced
4	sprigs rosemary
4	sprigs thyme
24	fresh green beans
12	baby carrots, halved lengthwise
1	small yellow squash, cut into 16 julienne pieces
½-¾	cup dry Vermouth
	Freshly ground pepper
	Fine sea salt

- Preheat oven to 375 degrees or grill to high.

- Cut four sheets of parchment, about 18 inches long and then fold each in half lengthwise. Cut each in a ½ heart shape, which will make a heart when fully open.

- Working on ½ of the heart, layer as follows:

  Potatoes

  Chicken breast

  Garlic, rosemary and thyme

  6 green beans

  4 pieces carrot

  4 pieces yellow squash

- Sprinkle with salt and pepper, and add vermouth.

- Fold the parchment in half and crimp edges to seal tightly. Bake 25 to 30 minutes.

VARIATION:

Foil can be used in place of parchment paper. If using foil,
can be cooked on preheated outdoor grill.

Lemon Chicken

If you love lemons you must make this dish.

Serves 4   Equipment: meat pounder, 10 to 12-inch sauté pan

4	boneless skinless chicken breasts
½	cup Wondra flour
	Pinch fine sea salt
	Freshly ground pepper
	Olive oil
3	cloves garlic, minced
1	cup dry white vermouth or dry white wine
	Juice of 1 lemon
10	ounces frozen artichokes, quartered
¼	cup chopped fresh basil
1	lemon, sliced thinly into rounds

- **Pound chicken to ¼-inch thickness. Set aside.**

- **Place flour in large bowl and season with salt and pepper.**

- **Thinly film sauté pan with olive oil and sauté chicken on one side until golden. Turn chicken and sauté other side. Add garlic in between chicken pieces.**

- **When chicken is golden on both sides, add vermouth and lemon juice. Turn heat to low and add artichokes and basil. Add lemon slices and simmer 10 minutes.**

SERVING SUGGESTION:

Serve over spinach linguine.

COOK'S TIP:

Wondra, commonly known as instant flour, is a very fine granular flour that is also used to make smooth sauces. All-purpose flour can be substituted.

Chicken in a Light Herb Cream Sauce with Artichokes, Peas and Garlic

A light herb cream sauce can be as satisfying as its heavier cousin.

Serves 4   Equipment: meat pounder, 10 to 12-inch sauté pan

4	boneless, skinless chicken breasts
	Fine sea salt
	Freshly ground pepper
1	cup flour
	Olive oil
4	cloves garlic, minced
½	cup fresh basil, chiffonade
½	cup Italian parsley, chopped
1	shallot, minced
10	ounces frozen artichoke hearts, defrosted enough to break apart
10	ounces petit peas
½	cup chicken stock
12	ounces evaporated skim milk

- **Pound chicken to ¼-inch thickness. Season with salt and pepper. Dredge in flour.**

- **Heat sauté pan and add olive oil to thinly film bottom of pan.**

- **Add chicken and sauté 2 to 3 minutes on each side. Add garlic and sauté until fragrant, 1 to 2 minutes.**

- **Add basil, parsley, shallot, artichokes, peas, stock and evaporated skim milk. Cook on low to medium, just below the boil for 10 minutes.**

- **Serve over couscous, rice, pasta, or polenta.**

Chicken Marsala with Porcini Mushrooms

A great standby that is both easy and elegant.

Serves 4

Equipment: meat pounder, 10 to 12-inch sauté pan, aluminum foil or parchment paper, coffee filter placed inside strainer, strainer placed over a bowl

---

4	boneless, skinless, chicken breasts
2	eggs or 4 egg whites
	Fine sea salt
	Freshly ground pepper
2	cups dry bread crumbs, unseasoned
½	cup Parmigiano-Reggiano, finely grated
	extra virgin olive oil
1	cup dry Marsala wine
1	cup chicken stock
1	cup dried porcini mushrooms, rehydrated
4	quart saucepan

- Pound chicken breasts to ½-inch even thickness.

- Scramble eggs (or egg whites) with a pinch of salt and a few grindings of pepper.

- Mix bread crumbs with cheese and place on foil or parchment.

- Dip chicken in egg mixture and then in bread crumbs. You can press the mixture onto the chicken with your hands to ensure even coating. Set aside.

- To rehydrate the mushrooms: in a 4 quart saucepan, bring wine and stock to a boil and keep simmering on stove. Add porcini and simmer 5 minutes. Drain this mixture through the coffee filter and reserve liquid. Reserve porcini and chop into bite-size pieces. Place stock/wine back in pan and simmer. (The purpose of straining is to clear the liquid of any dirt that might have been on the porcini.)

- Heat sauté pan and thinly film with olive oil. When oil is hot, add chicken and brown until golden on each side.

- Add mushrooms and reserved wine and stock mixture. Cover and cook 10 to 15 minutes until chicken is done.

Chicken Breast Stuffed with Spinach and Sun-Dried Tomato

This stuffing can also be tossed with pasta for a vegetarian entrée.

Serves 4   Equipment: 10 to 12-inch sauté pan with lid

Stuffing:

	Extra virgin olive oil
½	cup finely chopped onion
2	tablespoons chicken or vegetable stock
2	cups chopped mushrooms
2	garlic cloves, finely minced
2	cups packed baby spinach leaves
2	tablespoons sun-dried tomatoes (not in oil), chopped
¼	cup fresh basil, chopped
2	tablespoons fresh orange zest
	Freshly ground pepper

Chicken:

4	boneless chicken breasts (with or without skin)
1	cup dry white wine or chicken stock
	Fine sea salt
	Freshly ground pepper

- In sauté pan, combine olive oil, onion, and stock. Cook, stirring over low heat, until onion is tender. This will take 3 to 5 minutes.

- Add the mushrooms. Cook until tender and moisture has evaporated, approximately 3 to 5 minutes.

- Add garlic and cook 1 to 2 minutes. Stir in spinach and cook, stirring until wilted, approximately 2 to 3 minutes.

- Add sun-dried tomatoes, basil, orange zest and a grinding of pepper. Mix well. Remove from heat. Cool. Remove from pan and refrigerate until ready to use.

- Cut a pocket in the fleshy side of your chicken breast. Season outside with salt and pepper. Stuff until very plump.

- Thinly film sauté pan with olive oil and brown chicken on one side. Turn. Add 1 cup additional stock or wine.

- Cover and cook until chicken is done, 10 to 15 minutes or until internal temperature reaches 160 degrees. Can be basted with pan juices while cooking.

Chicken Breast Stuffed with Spinach and Sun-Dried Tomatoes continued

SERVING SUGGESTIONS:

Serve with a good bread, couscous cooked in
chicken stock, and a green salad for an easy, elegant dinner.

COOK'S TIP:

Completed dish can be made ahead, frozen and reheated in the microwave.

Parmesan Chicken

These are grown-up chicken fingers but the kids will like them too.

Serves 4   Equipment: parchment paper or aluminum foil, baking sheet, 2 shallow bowls or pie plates

---

1	cup fresh bread crumbs
¼	cup grated Parmigiano-Reggiano
½	cup pignoli nuts, toasted and finely chopped
½	teaspoon fine sea salt
	Freshly ground pepper, to taste
4	egg whites
4	boneless skinless chicken breasts

- Line a baking sheet with parchment or foil.

- Preheat oven to 400 degrees convection oven, or 425 degrees standard oven.

- Mix bread crumbs, cheese, pignoli, salt and pepper together in pie plate.

- Place egg whites in another pie plate.

- Pound chicken to even thickness, approximately ½-inch thick.

- Dip chicken in egg white.

- Dip chicken in bread crumbs and place on parchment paper or foil. Bake in convection oven for 15 minutes or standard oven for 25 minutes or until meat thermometer reaches 160 degrees.

Chicken Breast Stuffed with Ricotta Salata & Fresh Basil

Ricotta salata, also known as dry ricotta, is a delicious smooth, firm sheep's milk cheese which can be grated. It is generally sold in chunks and is imported from Italy.

Serves 4   Equipment: boning knife, 10 to 12-inch sauté pan with lid

---

¼	cup bread crumbs
1¼	cups white wine, divided as ¼ cup and 1 cup
4	ounces ricotta salata, grated
½	cup fresh basil, chopped
½	cup fresh Italian parsley, chopped
	Fine sea salt
	Freshly ground black pepper
4	boneless chicken breasts, with skin and a pocket for stuffing
	Olive oil

- Soak bread crumbs in ¼ cup white wine.

- Mix grated ricotta salata with basil and parsley, add wine soaked bread crumbs. Season with salt and pepper.

- Stuff each chicken breast with ¼ of the cheese mixture. Season the outside with salt and pepper.

- Thinly film sauté pan with olive oil and brown chicken on both sides, skin side first. Turn chicken and add 1 cup wine to deglaze pan. Cover and cook until chicken is done, approximately 10 minutes.

COOK'S TIP:

To make pocket for stuffing:
Lay a piece of chicken breast on the cutting board.
Find the thicker side. Insert a long thin boning knife part way in order to create a "pocket." Do not cut all the way through.
Do not push knife blade through entire breast.

Bloody Mary Cornish Hens

This is a versatile recipe that can cooked on the grill or in your oven.

Serves 4 (½ hen per person)   Equipment: mixing bowl, large plastic bag for marinating, optional: baking sheet

2	Cornish hens, total weight 3 to 3½ pounds
2	cups tomato juice
½	cup roughly chopped Italian Parsley
6	garlic cloves, sliced into rounds
1	teaspoon celery salt
1	tablespoon Worcestershire sauce
¼	cup Vodka
	Juice of 1 lemon
1	tablespoon horseradish
½	teaspoon freshly ground mixed peppercorns
1	tablespoon extra virgin olive oil

- Clean hens. Cut through breastbone separating the hen into one flat bird.

- Mix together tomato juice, parsley, garlic, celery salt, Worcestershire, vodka, lemon juice, horseradish, pepper and olive oil. Marinade hens for several hours or overnight.

- Preheat grill. Brush grill to ensure clean surface.

- Place hens skin side up on grill and grill on medium with lid closed.

- Cook until internal temperature of 165 degrees. Turn hens after 20 minutes for so.

- Or place hens on baking sheet and cook as follows:
    * Regular bake - 400 degrees for 45 minutes to 1 hour
    * Convection bake - 375 degrees for 45 minutes

VARIATIONS:

Whole roasting chicken

Chicken parts

SERVING SUGGESTION:

Serve with couscous cooked in chicken stock or a small pasta such as orzo.

Golden Roasted Turkey Breast with Orange Zest, Spinach & Sun-Dried Tomato Stuffing

This stuffing is also great as a side dish or tossed with leftover pasta for a quick meal.

Serves 4   Equipment: 10 to 12-inch sauté pan, roasting pan

Stuffing:

1	tablespoon extra virgin olive oil
½	cup finely chopped onion
2	tablespoons chicken or vegetable stock
2	cups chopped mushrooms
2	garlic cloves, finely minced
2	cups packed baby spinach leaves
2	tablespoons sun-dried tomato (not in oil), chopped
1	teaspoon grated orange zest
¼	cup fresh basil
	Freshly ground pepper

1-1¼	pounds boneless turkey breast with skin, (Turkey London broil)

- In sauté pan combine olive oil, onion, and stock. Cook, stirring over low heat, until onion is tender. This will take about 5 minutes.

- Add the mushrooms and cook stirring until tender and moisture has evaporated, approximately 3 to 5 minutes.

- Add garlic and cook about 1 minute. Stir in spinach and cook, stirring until wilted, about 1 minute.

- Add sun-dried tomatoes, orange zest, basil, and a grinding of fresh black pepper. Remove from heat. Cool.

- Stuff under the skin of turkey breast. Place in roasting pan and pour 1 cup additional stock or wine over turkey breast. Refrigerate until ready to roast.

- Roast in a 375 degree convection oven (25 to 30 minutes) or a 400 degree standard oven (40 to 45 minutes) until internal temperature reaches 165 degrees. Can be basted with pan juices every 10 minutes.

COOK'S TIP:

Slice like a London broil so that you get layers of turkey, stuffing, and golden brown skin.

Turkey Breast Stuffed with Wild Rice, Fruit and Herbs

Prepare wild rice a day or two in advance for quick preparation on the day you serve this special dish.

Serves 4 to 6

Equipment: 2 quart casserole dish with lid for stuffing, roasting pan with rack for turkey, meat pounder, twine

---

Wild Rice Stuffing:

1	cup wild rice
3	tablespoons minced shallots
1	bay leaf
¼	teaspoon fine sea salt
3	cups chicken stock
½	cup chopped mixed fresh herbs, such as thyme, Italian parsley, chives, rosemary, sage
1	cup chopped dried fruit such as apricots and cherries
1	cup chopped nuts such as walnuts or pecans
	Freshly ground pepper

Turkey:

1½	pounds boneless turkey breast with skin
	Fine sea salt
	Freshly ground pepper

- Preheat oven to 375 degrees.

- Rinse rice under running water and pick out any grains that do not look good to you. Place rice, shallots, bay leaf, salt and stock in a 2 quart casserole with lid and bake for 1 hour. Remove bay leaf. Add herbs, dried fruit and nuts. Cook 30 minutes or until rice is tender.

- Preheat oven to 400 degrees.

- Place turkey breast on cutting board and butterfly. Pound to even thickness. Season with salt and pepper.

- Place stuffing over turkey breast and roll turkey breast to enclose. Tie at 3-inch intervals.

- Place on roasting rack and roast for approximately 45 to 60 minutes or until meat thermometer reads 155 to 160 degrees. Let rest at least 15 minutes before slicing.

Turkey Breast Stuffed with Wild Rice, Fruit and Herbs continued

COOK'S TIPS:

To butterfly turkey breast: lay the breast on a cutting board,
slice through the thickest past of the breast so that you end up with a split breast
that is still connected in the middle. The surface area of the butterflied breast will be
double the size and thinner than the original breast.

Stuffing can be used with chicken, turkey or pork and can be made a day ahead.

Duck Breast with Cognac Soaked Cherries

The earlier in the day that you rub this duck with the roasted garlic the better! It is great for a dinner party or a romantic evening.

Equipment: large plastic bag, small saucepan, 8-inch ovenproof sauté pan

1	pound Magret duck breast
2	tablespoons roasted garlic puree (see recipe for Roasted Garlic p. 26)
½	teaspoon fine sea salt
	Freshly ground pepper
½	cup brandy
½	cup cognac
¼	cup dried cherries
¼	cup chicken stock
	Olive oil

- Trim all visible fat from duck breast.

- Rub with garlic puree. Season with salt and pepper. Pour brandy into plastic bag. Add duck. Let stand in refrigerator until cooking time.

- Place cognac in small saucepan. Bring to boil. Add cherries, remove from heat. Let cherries steep in cognac while cooking the duck. This can also be done earlier in the day.

- Drain cherries from cognac. Reserve cognac for sauce. Reserve cherries for finishing the dish.

- Preheat oven to 400 degrees at least 15 minutes prior to sautéing the duck.

- Heat sauté pan. Drain duck and pat dry. Lightly film the pan with olive oil. Add duck and sear on both sides.

- Place sauté pan in the center of your oven and roast until your meat thermometer reads 125 degrees, check doneness after 10 minutes. Remove from oven and place duck breast on cutting board to rest for a minimum of 10 minutes.

Duck Breast with Cognac Soaked Cherries continued

- **Using the same sauté pan, add the drained and reserved cognac, the chicken stock and return pan to medium heat. Heat the cognac/stock mixture on high to deglaze the sauté pan. Cook until the sauce reduces slightly and becomes more syrupy.**

- **Slice the duck breast on a diagonal, plate and pour the cognac over. Garnish with the cherries.**

VARIATION:

This recipe can also be used for a shell steak instead of duck breast.

COOK'S TIP:

This dish is nice served with a salad of mixed baby greens with a
balsamic vinaigrette, walnuts and crumbled blue cheese, and oven-roasted white
and sweet potatoes or wild rice.

Marinating the duck breast all day will add great flavor and make this a "do-ahead" recipe.

Pork Cutlets with Champagne Mustard and Sautéed Apples

This is a nice dish to prepare in the fall when apples are crisp and juicy.

Serves 4   Equipment: 2 (8 to 10-inch) sauté pans with 1 lid, grater or zester (for nutmeg)

4	boneless pork chops, approximately ½-inch thick
	Fine sea salt
	Freshly ground pepper
4	Granny Smith apples
1	tablespoon unsalted butter
1	lemon, juiced
½	teaspoon ground cinnamon
2	tablespoons light brown sugar
	Whole nutmeg
	Olive oil
1	tablespoon butter
½	cup cider or apple juice
1	small onion, finely chopped
1	clove garlic, minced
	Champagne mustard, approximately ¼ cup
½-1	cup dry white wine
2	teaspoons Knorr beef broth or concentrated broth
	Worcestershire sauce

- Season both sides of pork with salt and pepper. Set aside.

- Slice apples ¼-inch thick and sprinkle with lemon juice to retard browning. Season with cinnamon, sugar and a fresh grinding of nutmeg.

- Thinly film one sauté pan with olive oil and add butter. Sauté apples until tender but still firm. Add cider and simmer while cooking pork chops.

- Heat olive oil in another large sauté pan. Add pork and sauté until browned on both sides. Spread champagne mustard on top of cutlets.

- Sprinkle garlic and onions around chops. Add ½ cup white wine around chops.

- Add beef broth and Worcestershire. Stir to blend all ingredients around chops.

- Cover and cook until onions are softened, about 5 minutes.

- Serve with sautéed apples on the side.

COOK'S TIP:

Quick cooking rice can be added to the pork chop pan for a complete meal.

Pork Tenderloin with Mediterranean Crust

This recipe was developed so that you could have lots of flavor in every bite without the added chore of making sauce.

Serves 4 to 5   Equipment: roasting pan, butcher's twine

1¼-1½ pounds pork tenderloin

¼   cup stone ground Dijon mustard

2   tablespoons dry marjoram

2   tablespoons dry basil leaves

4-6   cloves garlic, finely minced

½   teaspoon fine sea salt

       Freshly ground pepper

- Preheat oven to 375 degrees.

- Tuck narrow end of tenderloin under the thicker part and tie for even cooking.

- Coat pork with Dijon mustard. Set aside.

- Mix seasonings, garlic, salt and about 5 grinds of fresh pepper. Coat pork tenderloin.

- Roast in preheated oven until meat thermometer reaches 150 to 160 degrees. Let rest 10 minutes before slicing.

- Serve.

Stuffed Flank Steak with Herb Stuffing and Mushroom Sherry Sauce

Many years ago, I won a cooking contest with this recipe-which I owe to a dear friend for giving me the idea.

Serves 6   Equipment: butcher's twine, plastic bag

1½-2   pounds flank steak, butterflied and cut into 2 pieces

1   recipe Mushroom Sherry Sauce (p. 20)

Stuffing:

2   cups fresh bread crumbs

2   shallots, finely minced or 2 cloves garlic, finely minced

¼   cup fresh Italian parsley

½   cup fresh basil

1   cup fresh spinach, chopped

1   cup fresh mushrooms, thinly sliced

¼   cup fresh oregano

½   cup Parmigiano-Reggiano

¼-½   cup red wine, such as Chianti or Sangiovese

Marinade:

1   cup dry red wine, such as Chianti or Sangiovese

¼   cup olive oil

2   garlic cloves, crushed

      Fine sea salt

      Freshly ground pepper

1   tablespoons Worcestershire sauce

Garnish:

      Additional fresh herbs

      Nasturtium flowers

Stuffed Flank Steak continued

- Preheat grill or grill pan.

- Mix all stuffing ingredients together and spread over each piece of flank steak. Roll and tie.

- Mix all marinade ingredients together. Place flank steaks in plastic bag and add marinade. Marinate in the refrigerator for several hours.

- Drain marinade from steaks.

- Grill to desired doneness. Slice into very thin rounds and place on platter, garnish with fresh herbs and nasturtium flowers.

COOK'S TIP:

If time permits marinate the unstuffed meat overnight.

Notes

Stress Free
Vegetables &
Vegetarian Entrées

Asparagus with Orange Glaze

Equipment: grater or zester, shallow casserole dish

½ cup fresh orange juice
Zest of 1 orange
1 tablespoon minced fresh ginger
(from approximately 1-inch of
fresh ginger)
2 teaspoons soy sauce
2 pounds fresh asparagus, trimmed

- Combine all of the ingredients except the asparagus. Mix well with a wire whisk.

- Wash asparagus and break ends off at point which they snap. Place the asparagus in a shallow ovenproof dish. Cover with the sauce and refrigerate for at least 2 hours, turning occasionally, if possible.

- Preheat the broiler. Broil the asparagus for 5 to 6 minutes or until tender. Be careful not to overcook.

- Serve immediately.

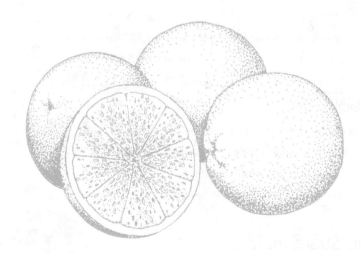

Easy Cheese Soufflé

This recipe brings back fond memories for me; it was one of my son David's favorites!

Yield: as many as 12 servings   Equipment: blender or food processor, soufflé dishes or muffin pans

---

6	eggs
½	cup evaporated skim milk
¼	cup grated Parmigiano-Reggiano
½	teaspoon Dijon mustard
½	teaspoon fine sea salt
¼	teaspoon freshly ground pepper
½	pound light Cheddar cheese, sharp recommended
11	ounces brick style Neufchatel cream cheese (light cream cheese)
	Nonstick cooking spray

- **Preheat oven to 375 degrees.**

- **In a blender or food processor, place the eggs, evaporated milk, Parmigiano, mustard, salt and pepper. Blend until smooth.**

- **With blender or processor running, break off pieces of cheddar and add to the work bowl. Next break off chunks of cream cheese and add to work bowl. After all cheese is incorporated, blend at high speed for 5 seconds.**

- **Spray a 4-cup soufflé dish or equivalent deep baking dish with nonstick cooking spray. You can also make 12 individual soufflés in muffin pans. Fill the soufflé dishes or pans to just below the rim and place in the oven.**

- **Bake until puffed and golden: large soufflé for 45 minutes**
  small for 15 to 20 minutes

COOK'S TIPS:

Batter can be made early in the day and refrigerated until baking time.

If using individual soufflé dishes, place on baking sheet for easier handling.

Surface may crack during baking and will add to appearance.

Soufflés can be held for a few minutes with oven door ajar. Like Risotto, soufflés do not wait long.

SERVING SUGGESTION:

Serve individual soufflés atop the Tre Colore Salad (minus the Gorgonzola) found on p. 70.

Garlic Mashed Potatoes

Serves 6 to 8   Equipment: saucepan , colander placed in large bowl, electric mixer

12 Yukon Gold potatoes, peeled and cut into 1-inch cubes	• Place potatoes, garlic and salt in heavy saucepan, add stock and additional water to cover.
6 cloves garlic, peeled	
1 teaspoon fine sea salt	• Boil until potatoes are fork tender.
4 cups chicken, vegetable or beef stock	• Drain liquid from potatoes into a bowl and reserve to add back to potatoes.
Freshly ground pepper, to taste	• Place potatoes in mixer bowl. Mix until smooth and add the hot cooking liquid until potatoes are desired consistency.

Healthy Note:

You have saved all the vitamins and minerals by
using the cooking liquid! Also, by using the cooking water you will retain
the potato starch, which will add richness to the dish.

Cook's Tip:

Leftover cooking liquid can be used in sauces or soups.
These potatoes can be frozen in an ovenproof casserole dish, defrosted and reheated
in a 350 degree oven until piping hot, approximately 45 minutes.

Mashed Potatoes with Asiago Cheese and Garlic

Serves 6 to 8   Equipment: heavy saucepan, colander placed in large bowl, mixer

12	Yukon Gold potatoes, peeled and cut into 1-inch cubes
4-6	cloves garlic
3	cups chicken, vegetable or beef stock
1	teaspoon fine sea salt
	Freshly ground pepper
1	cup grated Asiago Cheese

- Place potatoes, salt and garlic in heavy saucepan and add stock and additional water to cover.

- Boil until potatoes are fork tender.

- Drain liquid from potatoes into a bowl and reserve to add back to potatoes.

- Place potatoes in mixer bowl. Mix until smooth and add the hot cooking liquid until potatoes are desired consistency.

- When potatoes are smooth and creamy, mix in the Asiago cheese.

- The potatoes can be placed in a serving dish and covered until serving time.

Roasted Eggplant with Spinach Pesto

Serves 4   Equipment: food processor, baking sheet lined with parchment paper

4	cups fresh spinach
1	cup fresh Italian parsley
¾	cup grated Parmigiano-Reggiano, plus extra for garnish
6	cloves garlic
½-1	cup chicken or vegetable stock
2	baby eggplant, white or purple
	Olive oil

• **Preheat oven to 400 degrees.**

• **Cut eggplants in half lengthwise. Brush with olive oil, then place on baking sheet lined with parchment paper and roast in 400 degree oven for 20 to 30 minutes or until soft.**

• **Place spinach, parsley, Parmigiano-Reggiano and garlic in food processor and process until smooth. Add stock to achieve desired consistency. Set pesto aside.**

• **Spread spinach pesto on top of eggplant and garnish with a light sprinkling of Parmigiano-Reggiano. Place under broiler to warm pesto and brown cheese.**

Roasted Garlic Potatoes with Fresh Herbs

Serves 6 to 8   Equipment: large baking sheet, parchment paper, garlic peeler

3-4   pounds baby potatoes such as
        Yukon gold or red bliss
2   tablespoons fresh rosemary
8-10 very large cloves of garlic
        Extra virgin olive oil
        Fine sea salt
        Fresh ground pepper
¼   cup chopped Italian Parsley

- Preheat oven to 425 degrees.

- Wash and dry potatoes. Cut into uniform size pieces.

- Strip rosemary from stems. Slightly bruise with chef's knife.

- Peel garlic.

- Line baking sheet with parchment paper. Place potatoes, rosemary and garlic on baking sheet. Drizzle with just enough olive oil to thinly film all potatoes.

- Toss with salt and pepper.

- Roast in oven 45 minutes to 1 hour or until fork tender.

- Sprinkle with parsley and serve.

COOK'S TIP:

Regular sized potatoes can be used if cut into bite-size pieces.

133

Grilled Fruit and Vegetable Platter with Balsamic Drizzle

This vegetable platter makes a lovely centerpiece for a summer buffet table. Consider your grill when slicing vegetables and cut them so that they will not fall through the grate. Varying the vegetable types and sizes will add to the appearance of your platter. Grilling fresh fruit enhances the flavor.

Serves 6 to 8   Equipment: grill pan or outdoor grill, pastry brush, large platter, small saucepan

---

1	cup balsamic vinegar	1	large pineapple, cored and cut into slices
1	tablespoon honey	1	lemon, juiced
1	tablespoon fresh orange juice	4	ounces water
1	large eggplant, unpeeled and sliced into ¼-inch thick rounds	2	Granny Smith apples, cored, sliced and dipped in acidulated water (see Cook's Tips on next page)
2	medium zucchini, unpeeled and sliced lengthwise ¼-inch thick		Olive oil
2	sweet onions, peeled and sliced into very thin rounds	2	bulbs garlic, sliced in half through the center so that you have 4 round halves
1	red bell pepper, cored and sliced into ¼-inch rounds		Fine sea salt
1	green bell pepper, cored and sliced into ¼-inch rounds		Freshly ground pepper
1	yellow bell pepper, cored and sliced into ¼-inch rounds		Fresh basil for garnish

Grilled Fruit and Vegetable Platter continued

- **Preheat grill.**

- **Place vinegar and honey in small saucepan and cook for 15 to 20 minutes until reduced to ½ cup. Add orange juice.**

- **Brush all vegetables (including garlic) lightly with olive oil or place in large bowl and toss with olive oil. Place on grill and cook to desired doneness. Season with salt and pepper as soon as vegetables are done. Fruit can be grilled without olive oil.**

- **Mix together lemon juice and water.**

- **Drizzle honey/vinegar mixture over fruit and vegetables. Garnish with fresh basil sprigs and grilled garlic.**

COOK'S TIPS:

Some vegetables only require grilling on one side.
Heat kills vitamins and minerals, so the crispier the better.
Thinly sliced potatoes are nice on the grill.
Can be made a day ahead.

Acidulated water:
water to which a small amount of acid such as lemon juice
or vinegar is added to prevent discoloration of items such as apples and bananas.

Steamed Vegetable Melange with a Cheese Sauce

Serves 4 to 6   Equipment: saucepan with steamer insert, 4 quart saucepan

Vegetable Mix:

1	cup broccoli florets
1	cup cauliflower florets
1	cup baby carrots
4-6	Yukon gold potatoes, sliced ¼-inch
1	cup green beans, trimmed
1	lemon, sliced
6-8	chives
¼	cup Italian parsley, chopped

Cheese Sauce:

1	tablespoon canola oil or margarine
2	tablespoons flour
1-2	cups vegetable cooking liquid
½	cup grated cheese - your choice

- Layer vegetables in steamer basket and steam about 10 minutes. Serve with lemon and herb garnish.

- For cheese sauce, heat oil or margarine in a saucepan and add flour. Cook 2 to 3 minutes. Add cooking liquid. Whisk until smooth and thickened. Remove from heat and add cheese. Serve over vegetables.

VARIATION:

In place of cheese sauce, lightly sprinkle with grated cheese or top with a cream sauce.

COOK'S TIP:

Save the cooking water for soups, stews, sauces and casseroles.
It can be frozen or placed in a pitcher in the refrigerator for up to 1 week.

Black Bean and Corn Roll-Ups with Gazpacho Salsa

Serves 6 to 8

Black Bean and Corn Roll-Ups:

2	ears fresh corn or 1 cup frozen, defrosted
30	ounces canned black beans
½	cup red onion, chopped
1	lime, juiced
1	tablespoons canola oil
½	cup chopped cilantro, plus additional for garnish
1	tomato, chopped
½-1	teaspoon ground cumin
	Fine sea salt
	Freshly ground pepper
1	package flour tortillas
1	lime, quartered

Gazpacho Salsa:

1	green bell pepper, chopped
1	red bell pepper, chopped
4	inch cucumber, chopped
1	medium tomato, chopped
1	garlic clove, minced
1	tablespoon olive oil
1	tablespoon red wine vinegar

Roll-Ups:

- Cut corn from cob.

- Drain black beans and rinse until water runs clear.

- Mix black beans, corn, onion, juice of 1 lime, canola oil, tomato and cumin together. Add salt and pepper to taste.

- Place black bean mixture in center of tortilla. Roll up and place seam side down on serving platter. Top with Gazpacho Salsa. Garnish with fresh cilantro and lime wedges.

Gazpacho Salsa:

- Mix all gazpacho ingredients together. If possible make ahead and let flavors blend. Spoon over roll-ups.

COOK'S TIPS:

Tortillas come in a variety of sizes, therefore, depending on the tortillas selected, yield may vary.

The filling and salsa can be prepared one to two days ahead and refrigerated. Do not fill tortillas until close to serving time or they will get soggy.

Really fresh corn does not need to be cooked.

Roasted Vegetable and Quinoa Strudel with Warm Shallot Vinaigrette

Quinoa (keen-wah) is a high protein grain and an ancient cousin to Amaranth.

Serves 6   Equipment: baking sheet lined with parchment paper, saucepan

---

Strudel:

1	package frozen or fresh phyllo pastry (see Cook's Tip)
2	cups cooked quinoa (keen-wah), cooked according to package
2	cups chopped fresh vegetables such as zucchini, mushrooms, red bell pepper and onion
2	cloves garlic, peeled
½	cup chopped basil
¼	cup freshly grated Parmigiano-Reggiano
	Olive oil
	Cooking spray

Warm Shallot Vinaigrette:

3	tablespoons olive oil
2	tablespoons white wine vinegar
2	teaspoons honey
1	chopped shallot

- Preheat oven to 425 degrees.

- Thaw frozen phyllo dough in refrigerator for 3 hours or overnight.

- Roast vegetables and garlic in a hot oven until soft. To roast vegetables-place on sheet pan lined with parchment paper and toss with small amount of olive oil. Bake 425 degrees for 20 to 30 minutes. Cool vegetables. Mix vegetables with quinoa. Add basil and Parmigiano-Reggiano.

- Lay phyllo out near your work surface and cover with a damp towel.

- Take one sheet of phyllo and lay it on top of a baking sheet. Spray with cooking spray. Repeat this process with 5 sheets of phyllo.

- Spread mixture over dough leaving a 2-inch edge all around. Fold in short sides and begin rolling like a jelly roll. Place seam side down on baking sheet. Spray again with cooking spray. Wipe excess from baking sheet.

- Bake at 400 degrees for 30 minutes or until golden brown and beautiful.

Roasted Vegetable and Quinoa Strudel continued

- **Serve with Warm Shallot Vinaigrette. Heat olive oil, add white wine vinegar, honey and shallot. Mix well and keep warm for drizzling over strudel.**

COOK'S TIP:

Defrost frozen phyllo in the refrigerator for at least 3 hours.

Tamale Casserole with Cheddar Crust

This dish is a crowd pleaser and a little bit different.

Serves 8   Equipment: 13 x 9 x 2-inch baking dish, non-stick skillet

Filling:

1	tablespoon olive oil
1	medium green bell pepper, diced
1	medium onion, chopped
15	ounces canned pink beans, rinsed and drained well
15	ounces canned small white beans, rinsed and drained well
15	ounces canned chickpeas, rinsed and drained well
2½	teaspoons ground cumin
¼	teaspoon ground coriander
½	teaspoon dried oregano
½	teaspoon freshly ground pepper
28	ounces canned crushed tomatoes
½	cup medium hot salsa
½	cup sliced pimiento stuffed green olives

- Preheat oven to 375 degrees.

- Spray a 13 x 9 x 2-inch baking dish with cooking spray.

To prepare filling:

- In a heavy non-stick skillet, heat oil over medium high heat. Add the pepper and onion and sauté 6 to 8 minutes, or until the vegetables begin to soften. Add the beans. Toss well. Cook another 3 minutes for flavors to blend.

- Stir in the cumin, coriander, oregano, and pepper and sauté, stirring for about 30 seconds. Add the tomatoes, salsa, olives and ¼ cup water and bring to a boil. Remove from the heat and pour into prepared baking dish.

Tamale Casserole with Cheddar Crust continued

Crust:

1½	cups yellow cornmeal
1	cup all-purpose flour
1	teaspoon baking powder
½	teaspoon baking soda
¼	teaspoon salt
1¼	cups plain, low-fat yogurt
2	large eggs or 4 egg whites
2	tablespoons olive oil
1	cup low fat Cheddar cheese, shredded
½	cup chopped green onions
	Cooking spray

To prepare crust:

- In a large bowl, mix together cornmeal, flour, baking powder, baking soda and salt. Set aside.

- In another large bowl, whisk together the yogurt, eggs and oil until well blended. Stir in ¾ cup Cheddar cheese and the green onions. Pour the yogurt mixture over the cornmeal mixture and stir until blended. Spoon dollops of the mixture over the filling and spread evenly. Sprinkle with remaining ¼ cup Cheddar.

- Bake 25 to 30 minutes or until the filling is bubbly and the crust is lightly browned and firm. Cool a few minutes before serving.

Mixed Bean Chili with Polenta Triangles

This is a great vegetarian alternative to traditional chili.

Serves 8   Equipment: 8 quart soup pot, rubber gloves, sheet pan, saucepan

---

Chili:

1	teaspoon canola oil
1½	cups onion, chopped
2	large green bell peppers, chopped
2	celery stalks, sliced ½-inch thick
2	large carrots, sliced ½-inch thick
3	garlic cloves, minced
1	tablespoon minced jalapeño pepper (optional)
⅛	teaspoon cayenne pepper
2	teaspoons cumin
⅛	teaspoon ground cloves
2	teaspoons dried oregano
8	cups assorted beans, such as pinto, red kidney, white, chickpeas, pink
2	(28-ounce) cans diced tomatoes
½	cup chopped cilantro or Italian parsley
⅓	cup grated light Cheddar cheese for garnish
1	bunch scallions, sliced for garnish

Chili:

- Heat the oil in a large soup pot over medium high heat. Add the onion, pepper, celery and carrot and sauté until onion is translucent. Stir in the garlic, jalapeño, cayenne, cumin, cloves and oregano. Sauté 2 to 3 minutes.

- Add the beans, tomatoes, cilantro (or parsley) and bring to boil. Reduce the heat and simmer covered for 1 to 1½ hours or until flavors blend. Adjust seasonings before serving.

- Ladle into bowls and garnish with cheese and sliced scallions.

Mixed Bean Chili with Polenta Triangles continued

Polenta Triangles:

2	cups polenta or cornmeal
4	cups stock or water
1	cup shredded sharp Cheddar cheese
½	cup sliced scallions

Polenta Triangles:

- **Bring stock or water to boil. Whisk in polenta until smooth. Cook 5 to 10 minutes. Add cheese and scallions. Place in sheet pan and cool until firm. Cut into triangles and top chili.**

COOK'S TIPS:

Polenta can be made ahead and reheated before serving.

Wear rubber gloves when seeding and chopping the jalapeño.

Vegetarian Quesadilla with Roasted Corn Salsa

Yields 8   Equipment: 10 to 12-inch sauté pan, baking sheet

Mixed Bean Filling:

	Olive oil
3	cloves garlic, crushed and chopped
15	ounces canned pink beans, drained and rinsed
15	ounces canned small white beans, drained and rinsed
15	ounces canned black beans, drained and rinsed
½	cup cilantro, roughly chopped
4	plum tomatoes, chopped
½	cup red wine or vegetable stock
8	large flour tortillas

Roasted Corn Salsa:

1	ear fresh corn, kernels cut from cob
1	red bell pepper, chopped
½	cup cilantro, roughly chopped
1	clove garlic, crushed and minced
1	lime, juiced

- Preheat oven to 375 degrees.

- Thinly film sauté pan with olive oil. Add garlic and cook until slightly softened. Add beans, cilantro, tomatoes and wine and simmer 15 to 20 minutes. Mixture should be relatively dry so that it won't saturate tortillas.

- Lay each tortilla out and cover half of each tortilla with bean mixture. Fold tortillas and place on baking sheet. Heat in oven 10 - 15 minutes so that tortillas can brown and mixture will be piping hot. Cut into wedges and top with Roasted Corn Salsa.

- To prepare the Roasted Corn Salsa: Heat a large sauté pan, dry. Add corn and roast over high heat by shaking pan. When corn begins to brown, add pepper, cilantro, garlic and lime juice and cook 5 minutes.

Stress Free

Desserts

Apple Tarts

This could be considered a low-fat apple pie.

Equipment: 10 to 12-inch sauté pan, muffin tins, biscuit cutter

---

¼   cup unsalted butter

¼   cup brown sugar

2   pounds Granny Smith apples, peeled and chopped

¼   cup currants

½   cup apple brandy

1   box phyllo dough, defrosted at least 3 hours in refrigerator

Nonstick cooking spray

- Preheat oven to 350 degrees.

- Melt butter in sauté pan. Add brown sugar. Add apples and cook until tender. Add currants and brandy and cook 5 minutes. Cool.

- Make phyllo cups: Lay phyllo out near your work surface and cover with a damp towel. Take one sheet of phyllo and lay it on top of a baking sheet. Spray with cooking spray. Repeat this process with 4 sheets of phyllo. Cut phyllo slightly larger than muffin cups (a biscuit cutter can be used) and place a section of phyllo in each muffin cup.

- Bake in 350 degree oven for 8 to 10 minutes, until golden brown. Cool.

- Spoon the apple mixture into each cup and serve immediately.

COOK'S TIP:

Phyllo cups can be made ahead and kept frozen until ready to use,
but make sure that you place in a crush proof container.

SERVING SUGGESTION:

Add a dollop of frozen vanilla yogurt.

Apple Crunch Cake

This recipe was inspired by a cake a friend of mine made, which was called a Martha Washington Cake.

Serves 12 to 16   Equipment: 10-inch tube pan

2	cups plain, low-fat yogurt
2	eggs or 4 egg whites
1	teaspoon vanilla
2	cups all-purpose flour
¾	cup sugar
1	teaspoon baking powder
1	teaspoon baking soda
½	teaspoon fine sea salt
1	cup walnuts, chopped
1	teaspoon cinnamon
2	cups unpeeled and chopped baking apples, see Cook's Tips
	Nonstick cooking spray

- Mix wet ingredients together.
- Mix dry ingredients together. Add apples and mix.
- Combine wet and dry, mixing just until moistened.
- Spray tube pan with nonstick cooking spray. Pour batter into pan.
- Bake at 350 degrees for 50 to 60 minutes.

COOK'S TIPS:

This is a very moist cake and should be
refrigerated after a day due to the active cultures in the yogurt.

Apples suitable for baking include McIntosh, Winesap, Rome, Empire and Granny Smith.

Sprinkle top with a mixture of cinnamon and sugar.

Mixing the apples with the dry ingredients will prevent them
from sinking to the bottom of the batter.

Chocolate Cream Cheese Roll with Fresh Berries and Cream

This is a compilation of several recipes that add up to a great dessert, especially when made several hours ahead.

Equipment: electric mixer, 15 x 10 x 1-inch jelly-roll pan, parchment paper, clean dish towel, food processor with steel blade, oval platter

---

⅓	cup all-purpose flour
⅓	cup Hershey's cocoa
¼	teaspoon baking soda
4	egg yolks
½	teaspoon vanilla extract
¾	cup granulated sugar, divided, ¼ cup and ½ cup
4	egg whites
1	(8-ounce) brick Neufchâtel cream cheese (light)
¼	cup honey
2	tablespoons almond liquor
2	cups raspberries or strawberries

- Preheat oven to 375 degrees.

- Line a 15 x 10 x 1-inch baking sheet with parchment paper.

- Stir together flour, cocoa and baking soda. Set aside.

- Beat egg yolks and vanilla in medium bowl on high speed of mixer for 5 minutes or until thick and lemon colored. Gradually add ¼ cup of the granulated sugar, beating on high speed until sugar is almost dissolved.

- Wash and dry beaters. Beat egg whites in large bowl on medium speed of mixer until soft peaks form (tips curl). Gradually add remaining ½ cup granulated sugar, beating until stiff peaks form (tips stand straight). Fold egg yolk mixture into beaten egg whites. Sprinkle flour mixture over egg mixture; fold in gently just until combined. Spread batter evenly in prepared pan.

- Bake 12 to 15 minutes or until cake springs back when touched lightly. Immediately loosen edges of cake from pan; turn cake out onto a towel sprinkled with powdered sugar. Roll up towel and cake, jelly roll style, starting from one of the cake's short sides. Cool on wire rack.

Chocolate Cream Cheese Roll continued

- **To prepare filling, mix light cream cheese with honey and almond liquor in food processor until smooth. Carefully unroll cake and spread filling.**

- **Slice berries, if large and place over filling.**

- **Roll cake and refrigerate until serving time. Garnish with fresh mint and additional berries, if desired.**

Banana Nut Crêpes

An easy way to get the feel of Bananas Foster.

Serves 4   Equipment: 10 to 12-inch sauté pan

2	tablespoons sweet butter
4	tablespoons walnut pieces
4	bananas, sliced
4	tablespoons rum
	Low-fat vanilla yogurt or vanilla or rum raisin ice cream
	Ready made crêpes or 1 recipe Basic Crêpes (p. 34)

• Melt butter in sauté pan. Add walnuts and toss in butter. Add bananas and cook 2 to 3 minutes until softened. Remove from heat and add rum.

• Place ¼ of banana mixture in center of crêpe. Roll and top with ice cream or yogurt, if desired.

Cheesecake Squares with Raspberries

Making cheesecake in this way will allow you to eat just a bite or two.

Equipment: 9 x 13-inch pan

Crust:

1¾	cups graham cracker crumbs
½	teaspoon cinnamon
½	cup melted butter

Filling:

3	well beaten eggs
2	(8-ounce) bricks Neufchâtel cream cheese (light), not whipped
2	tablespoons vanilla extract
1	cup sugar
¼	teaspoon fine sea salt
3	cups sour cream or plain low-fat yogurt

Topping:

1	pint blueberries
1	pint raspberries
	Fresh mint leaves

- Preheat oven to 375 degrees.

- **To prepare Crust: Mix graham cracker crumbs, cinnamon and melted butter together and press into 9 x 13-inch pan.**

- **To prepare Filling: Beat eggs, cream cheese, vanilla, sugar and salt until smooth. Blend in sour cream.**

- **Pour into pan and bake until set, approximately 25 to 30 minutes.**

- **Garnish with fresh raspberries, blueberries and fresh mint leaves. Cut into individual servings.**

COOK'S TIPS:

Running a knife around the edge of
pan after cake has cooled prevents cracking.

Cheesecake can also be prepared in 9-inch springform pan
and baked for 45 minutes, in individual tart pans. Cooking time
will vary depending on size of pan. Cook until set.

Fresh Fruit Tart with Oatmeal Walnut Crust

This crunchy fiber filled crust needs to be made in time to cool before adding the filling and fruit. But it is worth it!

Serves 8   Equipment: 9-inch pie or tart pan, food processor

Crust:

1	cup old fashioned rolled oats
¼	cup all-purpose flour
¼	cup ground walnuts
4	tablespoons cold unsalted butter
3	tablespoons honey
3	tablespoons water, or as needed

Filling:

1	(8-ounce) brick Neufchâtel cream cheese (light)
¼	cup honey

Topping:

2	pints fresh fruit, a mixture of berries is nice or any combination of your favorite fresh fruits-see Cook's Tip.

- Preheat oven to 350 degrees.

- Place oats, flour and nuts in food processor. Pulse to mix. Add butter and pulse until you have coarse crumbs. Add honey and pulse until mixture holds together. If the mixture seems to stiff to press into a tart pan, add a few drops of water.

- Very gently, press the mixture into the bottom and up the sides of a 9-inch pie or tart pan. Bake 12 to 15 minutes or until golden. Cool.

- To prepare filling, mix cream cheese and honey together in food processor then spread over cooled pie crust.

- Top with mounds of your favorite fresh fruit.

Fresh Fruit Tart continued

COOK'S TIP:

Bananas, apples and pears need to be dipped in
acidulated water to maintain freshness and prevent browning. Acidulated water is
water that has had a squeeze of fresh lemon or lime juice, or a tablespoon of vinegar added to it.
Spray your measuring cup with non-stick cooking spray when measuring honey or peanut butter.

VARIATIONS:

mixed berries
chopped mango and sliced kiwi
canned pineapple and mandarin oranges
Can also be made in individual tart pans.
Can be drizzled with melted chocolate.

Lemon Poppy Seed Cake

This old standby is made with no-guilt yogurt.

Equipment: 10-inch tube pan, blender, electric mixer

2	cups sugar
¼	cup canola oil
1	tablespoon lemon zest
2	tablespoons poppy seeds, divided
1	egg, lightly beaten
2	egg whites, lightly beaten
½	cup non-fat cottage cheese
½	cup plain non-fat yogurt (or lemon yogurt)
2½	teaspoons vanilla extract
2	cups all-purpose flour, plus additional to lightly dust pan
1	tablespoon baking powder
4	tablespoons light brown sugar
1½	teaspoons ground cinnamon
	Nonstick cooking spray

- Preheat oven to 350 degrees.

- In a large bowl, cream sugar, oil, zest and 1 tablespoon of poppy seeds. Add the egg and egg whites and mix completely.

- Put the cottage cheese in the blender until smooth. Combine with yogurt. Pour into mixing bowl and blend in sugar and oil mixture. Add vanilla.

- Slowly add the flour and baking powder, stirring until blended.

- Lightly spray a 10-inch tube pan. Pour ⅔ of batter into pan.

- In a small bowl, combine the brown sugar, cinnamon and remaining poppy seeds. Sprinkle over the batter. Pour in the remaining batter.

- Bake 40 to 45 minutes or until toothpick comes clean.

VARIATION:

Use lemon flavored yogurt for an extra dose of lemon.

Can be made in muffin tins; bake 15 to 20 minutes.

Mango Phyllo Tarts

For those times when a light bite is just right.

Equipment: muffin tins, food processor fitted with steel blade, baking sheet

2   soft mangoes, diced

1   (8-ounce) brick Neufchâtel cream cheese (light)

2   tablespoons honey

1   box phyllo dough, defrosted in refrigerator for 3 hours or overnight

    Cooking spray

- Preheat oven to 325 degrees.

- **Make phyllo cups: Lay phyllo out near your work surface and cover with a damp towel. Take one sheet of phyllo and lay it on top of a baking sheet. Spray with cooking spray. Repeat this process with 4 sheets of phyllo. Cut phyllo slightly large than muffin cups (a biscuit cutter can be used) and place a piece of phyllo in each muffin cup.**

- **Bake in 325 degree oven for 8 to 10 minutes, until golden brown. Cool.**

- **Mix cream cheese and honey. Place a small amount in the bottom of each phyllo cup.**

- **Top with chopped mango.**

HEALTHY NOTE:

Mango is a powerhouse of vitamin C. It is more highly concentrated than an orange.

Pumpkin Spice Ring

When I worked at The Chubb Fitness Center, we offered a recipe of the week and this was one of the features. It is a luscious, low-fat holiday dessert!

Serves 16   Equipment: electric mixer, 10-inch tube pan

1	teaspoon ground cinnamon
¾	teaspoon salt
½	teaspoon ground ginger
½	teaspoon ground nutmeg
1¼	cups cake flour
2	cups confectioners' sugar, divided, plus additional for dusting cake
12-14	large egg whites to equal 1⅔ cups
1½	teaspoons cream of tartar
1½	teaspoons vanilla extract
1	cup solid pack pumpkin (not pie mix)
	Cooking spray

- Preheat oven to 375 degrees.

- Mix cinnamon, salt, ginger, nutmeg, flour and 1 cup confectioners' sugar in a bowl and set aside.

- In large mixer bowl, beat egg whites and cream of tartar until soft peaks form; add vanilla. Beating at high speed, sprinkle in 1 cup (2 tablespoons at a time) confectioners' sugar, until sugar dissolves and whites stand in stiff peaks. Remove 1 cup egg whites to medium bowl and fold in pumpkin.

- With rubber spatula or wire whisk, fold flour mixture into beaten egg whites in large bowl just until flour disappears. Then, gently fold in pumpkin mixture. Do not overmix.

- Pour batter into 10-inch tube pan that has been sprayed with nonstick cooking spray. Bake 35 minutes or until cake springs back when lightly touched. Invert cake in pan on funnel or bottle; cool completely. This will keep cake from falling.

- Loosen cake from pan; place on serving plate and dust with additional confectioners' sugar.

Tiramisu Cake

This low-fat cake is a great summer dessert since it's not baked. You can even vary it by using a chocolate angel food cake!

Serves 12   Equipment: grater, serrated knife, 3 dinner plates

1	angel food cake
1	cup cold Espresso coffee
½	cup Amaretto liqueur
2	cups part-skim ricotta cheese
1	cup mascarpone cheese
¼	cup confectioners' sugar
1½	cups sliced almonds, toasted
1	ounce bittersweet chocolate

- Cut cake into 3 equal layers and place each on a dinner plate.

- In a small bowl, combine the coffee and amaretto. Spoon ⅓ of the mixture over each layer.

- In another bowl, mix together the ricotta, mascarpone and sugar until well blended. Divide cheese mixture into 3 equal portions.

- Place bottom layer on platter. Take 1 portion of cheese and cover first layer with ⅓ of this cheese mixture. Top with another layer and repeat process until all layers are stacked.

- Cover outside of cake with remaining cheese mixture. Press almonds onto top and sides of cake.

- Shave or grate chocolate over top.

VARIATION:
Use a chocolate angel food cake, fill it with the cheese mixture and fresh fruit.

COOK'S TIP:
Make a day or two ahead to let flavors blend and cake set.

Stress Free…

Notes

Stress Free…

Stress Free...

Lifestyle Designs

Barbara Seeling Brown
232 Spencer Rd.
Basking Ridge, NJ 07920

908-766-6957

or visit my website at: www.lifestyledesigns.com

Please send me _____ copies of *Stress Free Cooking*   @ $19.95 each _____

    Please add shipping and handling   @ $ 3.00 each _____

    New Jersey residents add 6% sales tax   _____

Name _____

Address _____

City _____ State _____ Zip _____

Make checks payable to *Lifestyle Designs*

- -

Lifestyle Designs

Barbara Seeling Brown
232 Spencer Rd.
Basking Ridge, NJ 07920

908-766-6957

or visit my website at: www.lifestyledesigns.com

Please send me _____ copies of *Stress Free Cooking*   @ $19.95 each _____

    Please add shipping and handling   @ $ 3.00 each _____

    New Jersey residents add 6% sales tax   _____

Name _____

Address _____

City _____ State _____ Zip _____

Make checks payable to *Lifestyle Designs*